QUEEN
GODDESS
OF THE
OFFICE

QUEEN GODDESS
OF THE
OFFICE

TAWNY MAE HARRIS

iUniverse

QUEEN GODDESS OF THE OFFICE

iUniverse books may be ordered through booksellers or by contacting:

iUniverse
1663 Liberty Drive
Bloomington, IN 47403
www.iuniverse.com
844-349-9409

ISBN: 978-1-6632-2913-7 (sc)
ISBN: 978-1-6632-2912-0 (e)

Print information available on the last page.

iUniverse rev. date: 09/16/2021

The Kiss

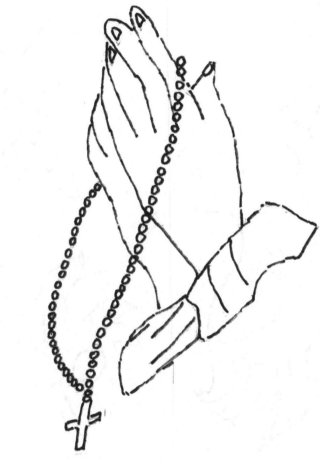

PRAY HARD

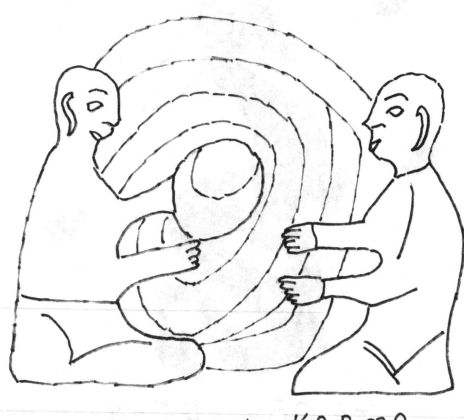

BUDDAH KARMA

GLORY DAYS
dedicated to
Meribah & Alison

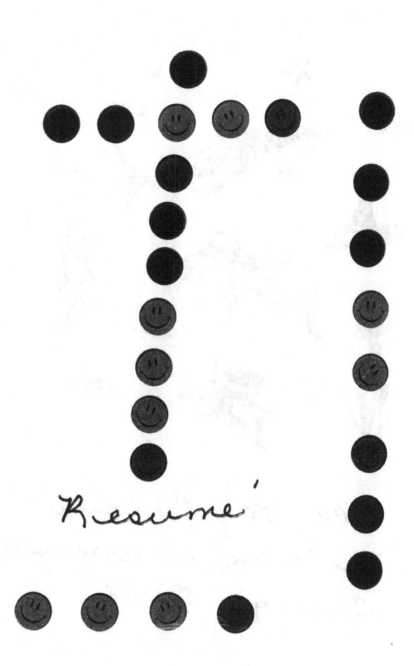

Resumé

All My Children
dedicated to Wrangler,
Theology, & Juju

CLOUD NINE

dedicated to
True / Trust / Truth
&
Forgiveness

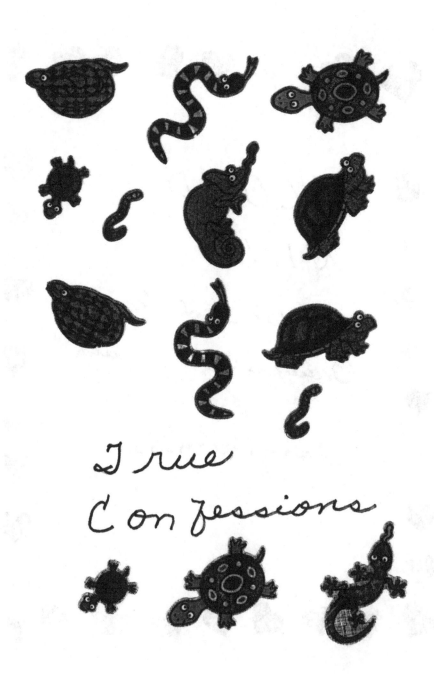

True
Confessions

SCREAM

FOR

ICE CREAM

Hebrew Tabernacle

GLORY DAYS

Kindergarten: Micah my gay brother & I made up. Do I really want him to eat shit & die? No, not really! I had a dream that Micah had a brain tumor & needed to exercise his head. I was driving a car. It was dark & the lights didn't work. I was walking my beloved German shepherd husky, Calvin Klein, that the jerk neighbor made me get rid of. I had to take her to the Humane Society. We were walking home & we had to go down these steps. A nice black lady offered me $15.00; but, I said no you keep it. You need it. We went to Hebrew Tabernacle Episcopalian Kindergarden. Micah threw a brush & gave me a black eye. The reverend said I would rather fight than switch. I loved that pastor! Open their eyes to see, ears to hear. An eye for an eye, a tooth for a tooth.

True/Trust/Truth my best Scorpio 9-11 girlfriend who died from a hoskiens tumor years ago & her Sagittarius husband, Aaron, had a son & a atheist daughter. Her son 6 years old child got attacked by 2 loose great danes. The darling grandson was walking down the street & had 100 stitches in his leg & 11 bites & is on morphine. He cannot walk & they are suing their asses off. The child is on the prayer list. Mae is also on the prayer list for home kidney dialysis. They treat me like a queen. 1st grade: I learned my ABC's alphabet, count to 100 & how to read. See Jane run. See Dick work. I got sent out in the hall for saying the letter "P." That is so ridiculous! I had the chicken pox & slit my vagina swinging on the black iron rails. It burned like hell when I peed. I slept in Mom's Loyal Dedication's bed & picked the scales of chicken pox out of my hair. The midget girl was my best friend. Micah was in the 1st grade & wrote come in & have a burbin. His rich 1st grade teacher who owned the Dairy Queen got stabbed to death 80 times by a nephew who wanted money. The love of money is the root of all evil.

??? All we did was read. The reverend's wife was the teacher & she sent me out in the hall for garling water. I was a dunce. I was answering the phone for the mean principal. The aron fell off the chair. A talented boy who is now a doctor said if you tell me what happened, I will tell you who Santa Claus is - your parents. A boy shit in the closet. I got hit in the head with a swing & my gay brother Micah laughed. We went to Gabes in Owensboro to swim & eat lobster. It was Mom's junkie nurse friend, Japan, & her 2 daughters China & Eternity. I was playing on the monkey bars & fell flat on my face bursting my nose & lip. Blood was coming out of my mouth & I had to have 3 stitches. The x-ray technician looked just like my favorite cousin, Job, who got arrested for selling oxycorten. I did not break my nose. We were in the emergency room for 3 hours. The doctor was playing golf & I could not swim. Hotels do not have a 13th floor. I hated school. I missed my grandmother seamstress, Wonderful Strength. I worshipped the ground she walked on. She was very wise. Mom, Loyal Dedication, used to slap us till our nose bled

& she beat us with a belt, was the worst alcoholic I have ever seen, & shot herself in front of us. She should have lost her children. She was onry & strong.

3rd grade: 8-25-20 Today is my grandmother's birthday & she was born in 1900 and died in 1972. She could not stand black men & drugs. My whole world crashed. I was 10 years old when I started my period. Menastrating so young. Mom Loyal Dedication threw pamphlets on me & my brother Micah made fun of me. "Tampoon! Tampoon!" I wanted to be a cheerleader. I hated SRA & learned how to cursive write. All I wanted to do is draw. The teacher had deformed fingers & toes.

4th grade: This was my favorite teacher. I finally enjoyed learning. Multiplication, dictionary races, division, auto harp, plays. The teacher had eyes in the back of her head. & we could not talk during lunch. Why? I do not like fat dresses. There was a retarded mentally challenged girl in our class named Gracie. Daughter of the moon Nacomis. How much wood can a wood chuck cut? The teacher had 2 sons. She fed one cod liver oil & he grew up big & strong. Her other son was scrawny. My hair was long & pretty. I misspelled the word guard. Mom was having parties & I could not study.

5th grade: I cut off all my hair & I looked so ugly. I had a lucky troll with yellow hair & the teacher took it away & was going to give it to her daughter. A smart pretty girlfriend whose husband & son both commited suicide, the saddest thing I ever heard, put grass in their mailbox & called them up banging pans on the phone. We had to write an apology note to the dumb doctor. I got sent out in the hall for laughing at Richard Nixon's nose. I was an artist. This black boy was stealing purses & got beat with a paddle. During recess, I tutored 3 poor, dirty children because I looked like a teacher. The principal was mean. Are you seeing & hearing things, Mae? Is it the end of the world?

Do you go to hell if you commit suicide? Do atheists go to hell? Wear black to funerals. I believe in abortion in rape, incest, & mental retardation.

6th grade: There are ghosts in my house. God is everywhere. Is Mae clairvoyant? Thank you for your persistant candle lighting faith. I AM coming down to save you from poverty & hate. This world is sick. There are pedifiles, psychopaths, & narcissis. Heaven is for real. Homosexuality is gross. Charity, my best girlfriend acts like her shit doesn't stink & wants my stimulus check. _____ her! Ecclesiastes says I have a big _____ing house, what does she have? You had better not covet & you had better not steal.

Mom Loyal Dedication broke my heart when she died at 65. Calling me a fat hog is the only time she apologized.

I cannot stand to look in the mirror God has blessed me with home kidney dialysis. I got my financial waiver. Cheer, my smart, funny black soul sister died from a disease unknown in a nursing home with a feeding tube. Penance. You could have sued Shop-a-Lot #666 #999. Angel I & Isabella died & went to Heaven #7. You had better get a sword. Peace, art teacher, mom's best beautiful friend died at 89. Jeremiah - why do you say peace when there is no peace? My halo is temporality out of order. How many times have you been raped? Pray for discernment & understanding. Is death a blessing? The wages of sin is death. Faith without good works is dead. Messiah, gay organist at Hebrew Tabernacle Episcopalian Church was full of good works.

Calm - not speed. Dream big! Claim big things! Think positive. Hope flourishes. Doubt flies.

Count your blessings was the only nice thing that mom said. I am not a greedy gut! I love my cat, Theology, a bushel & a peck & a hug around the neck. Why do men take advantage of women? Lorana Boblit is my hero. Look at that dick on that bug that splattered on the windshield. Fable, my best girlfriend at Zion, Egypt High School passed away. We used to do mescaline, Acid L.S.D. pot, & cocaine. God lifted that from me. I saw God spell on acid, blue microdot. It was awesome! Rainbow colors fly from your fingertips.

I am scared of purple rain & the dark. Charlie Daniels had better roison up that violin. I could not stand violin in the 6th grade. I broke the storm door glass window out with my violin case. I felt bad! I did not get in trouble - it was an accident. Now dead deceased gay lesbian alcoholic can see all the hell I go thru with kidney dialysis. Her name was Ecclesiastes which means star. She was a bitch! I threw puked my guts up last night. 1-25-21 It rained all day. I had to get my furnace fixed. I am so mad! Poor pitiful pearl. Why do we have to die? To be with God in eternity. Ecclesiastes died of a heart attack & she will get her revenge against happiness & joy. Vengeance is mine saith the Lord. I am off home kidney dialysis on Tuesdays & Saturdays. Hallelujah! Biden won! Amazing grace how great thou are who saved a wretch like me.

I once was lost but now am found was blind and now can see Alexis, my best girlfriend at Camel Carriers Trucking Company went blind from diabetes & died. We went to see the Chippendales, went out to eat, & frequented bars having fun. I loved her so much! She was so pretty! I can barely walk with this catheder in my stomach.

Aaron, True/Trust/Truth's Sagittarian husband is like a brother-in-law. Aaron is Jehovah Witness. His bitchy wife is Catholic and lost 2 young sons due to overdoses of heroin. We are not interested in sex. Beware of Scorpios! This 6th grade year we went to a different school. & said prayers & got whipped by paddles. I cannot stand to be touched by a girl. Persistance & her family went down to the lake, ate banana splits, sun bathed. You had better not swim with a black man. We used to trade I.D. bracelets for going steady & I made my first C in history. Laughter, my awesome step mother passed away at 91. She is with Dad Perseverence. You had better take the bitter with the sweet. Have I fallen out of grace? It's a dog eat dog world.

7th grade: This year I went out for cheerleader. Strawberry short cake, gooseberry pie. V-I-C-T-O-R-Y Do you think we'll win? I bet you we'll do & we'll make all those baskets too! We were good. We made 1st place in the district. I had a strict black teacher & we used to tumble & play dodge ball. Forgiveness & I are blood sisters. Beat the other team. Beat the other team now & we took showers & sang A-M-E-N in the hall.

We had a food fight with spaghetti & butter & got exspelled. The principal was going out with 15 year old prostitutes, accused me of trashing the bathroom. I didn't do it! He said we can do without one cheerleader. I could do one handed cartwheels, round offs, limbos, splits. I was good! Mae is Lee Lamb & she is the favorite. Meribah was the smartest, prettiest best cheerleader & died at 57. I loved her mother! Look at her hair. I had a 24 inch waist & my grandmother Wonderful Strength could have sewn our cheerleading uniforms. My grandmother said do not be with a black man. I did everything she said to do. She had gray hair & brown eyes, olive skin. So fight with your shadow. She was the wisest lady that ever lived. Mammy was the youngest of nine children & had 4 girls. I worshipped the ground she walked on - 8-25-1900. She drank buttermilk & cornbread & had a girlfriend that walked at night from the courthouse with a gun in her purse. She said her brothers were mean to her. She had a sister that commited suicide & said the man, her husband, was so mean he probably killed her. Mammy did not drink. She said it makes you silly. Beware of Virgos, Leos, & Pisces, Capricorns. It is Tuesday not Saturday. I am beginning to get confused. 1-26-21 I am scared of racoons. My neighbors are crazy! You had better not shoot or hang yourself. God has perfect timing. Every hair on your head is counted. You Mae & Rev. Daniels are going straight to Heaven. Jesus is coming back very, very soon.

Christ has died. Christ has risen. Christ will come again. Blessed are the poor. Tell the bitch Joy to get out of your house - Tara abode. My white cat with gold eyes Wrangler cannot stand you. Dr. Blessings is a beautiful kidney doctor. He is Indian & Indians are beautiful. He does not know what the world is coming to with COVID-19. The nice nurses are saints & treat me like a queen goddess. The beautiful red-headed social worker who is an angel says I better not croak. God Bless You! The nutritionist is the prettiest girl I have ever seen tiny with blonde hair & brown eyes & my protein is low. What if a child shut down your kidneys. The lithium shut down mine, you had better pray for these people. What do these dreams mean?

Kidney disease does not define you. You define it. The beautiful receptionist gave me a quiet, blue blanket, pajamas, jacket, cat toys. Keep sending them flowers! Heroes work here! You are with Ms. God. You promised me Heaven but put me thru hell. A school of hard knocks. A fool & his money is soon departed. Love the busy life. Praise is the devil's death knell. Mammy was Baptist & she did not wear pants- only black dress, a 50 bra & girdle. The math teacher sent me out in the hall for laughing. I was talking to a retarded boy & she said I would talk to anybody. We were learning sex education in science. We span the bottle & kissed in English class.

8th grade: My hair was long, blonde & metallic green from the chlorine from the country club swimming pool & sun-in. I went out for cheerleading. I was lucky #9. I dated Wonderful Advisor, the basketball star who gave me a sweetheart ring - puppy love. I should have stuck with him. We used to kiss - we were such a popular couple. He had blonde hair & brown eyes. In the ninth grade, my grandmother, Wonderful Strength died. I turned to wine & drugs. Germs, germs, germs. I started smoking Doral cigarettes & Lazerus's brother turned me on to pot, marihuana. Later, I did mescaline & acid. I got pregnant at 17 & Faith, my Pisces cousin aborted my child. Lazerus shot himself & died. Do suicides go to hell? I have been in jail. Monk, Lazerus is in a half-way house in heaven. The 2 aborted neonates are Alison Rain & Joshua (to kill) Alex. I graduated High School in 1976, bicentennial year after mom shot herself in front of us. I had a 3.4 g.p.a. Blood is everywhere. Count your blessings! I am so afraid of God. Where is your soul? I did angel dust (horse tranquilizer) & smoked a pipe. God saved me. I cannot stand pedifiles. This world is crazy. The rain drives me insane. You had better not do cocaine. Mae is a lover not a fighter, a coward. You have been slapped in the face till your nose bled & beat with a belt. You are a mother _____ing bitch, Mae.

Look what happened at Mammoth Cave. You released all the slaves. People are eating shit. You told Joy to get out of your house. Her son is atheist & atheists go straight to hell. You are wearing maroon, maroon & white, fight, fight. Watermelon, watermelon rhine, look at the scoreboard, see whose behind. Paul has aides & plays the piano. Sardines & oranges - sex toys. You had better not _____ him. You are a greedy gut. The devil's eyes are green. What if your child O'd? Praise God for another day. You have fallen out of grace. I am going to spit on your grave, Faith. Sprinkle, sprinkle fairy dust, bitch. What are you living for Mae? That is so mean. God is a great God. Those angels are answering calls just as fast as they can. Who are you? I AM. You cannot stand the name Sam. You cannot stand that black vice-principal. He is calling your mother at 821-1906 at the Real Estate office.

I am dutch & you'd better get these spiders off me. I o'd on valium & had to get my stomach pumped. I am on the 6th floor. Thorazine shuffle. Suicide is murder. Why does God hate me? God does not hate people. He loves everybody! God cannot stand snobs. You lost your job. You are a fat hog is the only time your mother apologized. I will never forgive her! She is a devil worshipper. Gift/gifted, my talented guitar player who died at 49 got busted for drugs. It's all her fault that I smoke. She was a good Pisces. Who is Aragon? Who is Gandalf? Hornets are bad, bad bugs!

You slit your wrist. Watch it bleed! You are petrified of needles. Enough is enough. You were hellians in Zion, Egypt High School. You are a bride of Jesus Christ, Mae. These are the end of days. You are scared of grizzley bears - the revenant. Shoot that bear! What would you do if they killed your son?

You had better say that Lords prayer. Mae is white trash. You have magic powers, Mae. It is snowing & you miss your German shepherd dog, Calvin Klein - Snowden Zodiac Spy. Did the dog die? Your girlfriend Lamb is a slut. She's got an EPO against her ex-boyfriend. Sorry shit, what did you do it for? Does the truth hurt? Satan I Ezekiel called you a jackass. How many years did his mother lie in bed with the disease manic-depression? Micah gives you the creeps. Brandy, you're a fine girl. What a good wife you would be, but, the love of my lady is the sea. God is a jealous God. LOVE is not jealous - my rainbow is overdue. Give me silver, blue, & gold - the color of the sky I am told. Pray hard! Albinos have pink eyes. Jesus is carrying you thru all these tests, trials & tribulations. Bell witch is dead. Keep yourself alive!

Tie a 100 yellow ribbons around that old oak tree for Fear who drowned.

Micah is a sissy. You cannot stand to be called spacey. Mae is a Christian. You have been called every name in the book - bitch, slut, whore. The only mean thing I ever did was throw a warty frog to see if it would be paralyzed. I cannot stand the name Colby. Season, Onyx & Fawn are the names of my dream girls. What if I had triplets? Now, at 63, I am hooked up to a kidney cycler for the rest of my life. Hide the knife. I had no idea what I was doing when cousin Faith took me to have an abortion. Tomb in the womb. It will only take 5 minutes. Faith is dead from breast cancer. She got to have her 5 children.

Mom Loyal Dedication did not want grandchildren. I did! Your mother was a bitch! How many times did St. Peter later rape you? Give St. Peter a candle & go straight to

Heaven. Who is that shiek guru? Eat fish the last 3 months of your pregnancy for brain food. Will Lazerus beat me - stairway to Heaven. I am so dizzy! I cannot stand the pain in my stomach, feet, & legs. Dr. Blessings is so compassionate just like my best girlfriend Ruthie that died from lung cancer at 52. She did not go to church but was saved, drank beer, smoked, collected gargoyls, dragons & was the sweetest, kindest person in the whole world. On my candle - fire, fire all aglow, tell me what you know.

Her ex-husband is a jerk, witchdoctor, did acid, sold meth, burned down a house collected insurance, stuck a gas line in a house because they would not pay $1000 for drugs, wanted to sleep in my basement, took all my dishes, wanted my furniture. Her son got arrested for meth, got the car, sold the trailor for $4000 & is in rehab. They had to get rid of the darling dauchsand dogs. Ruthie was a hippy & did not pray for money. They went to Woodstock & she was in House of Horrors/ubx mental hospital mental hospital for 5 days. I had to stay there a month & a half. Cauldron, cauldron forgive, forgotten. Will you be pardoned? That man makes me want to puke. Karma is going to get you, Mae. There is good karma & bad karma. Look what happened to John Lennon, the Beatles. The musician got shot & killed. I want my money for praying. I cannot stand beards & mustaches! It is very, very cold today 1-28-21 & the furnace was not working because of a loose fuse. - nore bad luck. It is bad luck to be born a duck. Religious Gabriel got fired from Shop-a-Lot #666 #999 for stealing. Get your own __ing drugs. She is on Prosac. I would be afraid I would kill somebody on that shit. I am on Geodon, Zyproxa, Levothyroxin, Eisiniphrie, Simvastin, Bi-carb, Zanex, & binders, Calcitrol. I do not want to kill anybody!

Mae is a hippy. Peace in the Middle East. Is this COVID-19 vaccine safe? What is this world coming to? Don't piss an Aquarius off! Cut out your tongue. Cruelty is my #1 pet peeve. In Zion, Egypt High school, I was cheerleader, in Pep Club, Beta Club, secretary-treasurer of art class. Those were the glory days in 1976. I graduated Zion, Egypt Community College in 1981 with 2 associate degrees in Arts (all the prerequites in R.N. Nursing, and Applied Science (secretarial administration, 2 who's who & a 3.6 g.p.a. I made 100% in medical terminology. I took psychology, sociology, English 101, 102, Speech, business, office management, shorthand, typing, accounting. One of the greatest teacher passed away. She could not say no in the mirror & got many students scholarships. I loved her! She was Episcopalian & very pretty with 2 sons. Her husband was a lawyer & died from lung cancer. I had to make-up incompletes & was in a play welcome to the Monkey House. 1981 was a good year!

I had to be tutored in accounting II. I made an A. I had an apartment that was furnished for $175 a month. The owner shot himself because he was in pain from cancer. Why did God make roaches? I had 3 jobs cleaning offices. Mom was the best boss, I ever had.

It's just like Jeckyl & Hyde drinking vodka & water. I had a baby turtle named Winky. Persistance & I were very promiscuous. Those were the good old days. Persistance is dead with 2 darling grown boys. Oh, how I mourn. We used to hop bars & pick up men. I got begged to death & raped by a fat man who wanted to marry me. Persistance had long saggy titties & should have moved to Nebraska. She got the good-looking man. We had to hide the knife from this girl who got an abortion. Mom was so dissappointed when she visited me. That's when I had my beloved sheepdog, LEVI. I snuck her in the upstairs apartment. I drank wine & burned a hole in my best girlfriend's mother's blanket with a drunken cigarette. I made her a beautiful Afghan to make up for it. Robin Williams was manic-depressive & hung himself. Did he go to hell for that? I loved Mork & Mindy. Na-nu. Na nu. A rich person going up to Heaven is like a camel going thru an eye of a needle. Everything in Revelations is coming true. We are doomed. Look at the bloody moon. St. Jude represents the sign of Aquarius. The devil made your mother shoot herself. You had better smile per Aunt Beautiful Patience. You had better do everything in your power to stay alive. Dead people are alive & resurrected per Rev. Daniels. If you fart at the table, your mother will stab you with a fork. You had better be careful what you wish for. You have a chemical imbalance in your brain & it races & gets off track per Dr. Sweden at Our Lady of Mercy, a Catholic mental hospital. Control your stuff. - pussy control. You are not a __ing french fry. You cannot stand Bartholomew. Guess what, chicken snot. You shuffled the smiley face cards - the Guardian. All you got was a hat from your father. You make your mother sick. You cannot stand your parents. When your mother & father forsake thee, then I will lift you up. You are _____ed up in the head, Mae. You are not going to hell. Pull up your bootstraps & go on. You have been tested way too hard.

God on a harley. You ask too many questions. Starsky Michelle Mystique. God wants you to eat. Every thing will be alright. You are a lover not a fighter. Uncle Protection almost raped me - I am not Baba! He had a farm in Concordia, $30,000 & all I got was a ring, dishes, & Chantilly silverware which I sold the silverware for $750 to Faith & bought 2 expensive pictures - $350 a piece. I get my first COVID-19 vaccine tomorrow. And I had better not lose my car. These boots are made for walking & I'll tell you what to do. One of these days these boots are going to stomp all over you. Where is that truck that says God's legacy? Charity is jealous of you because of money. I wish I could get off kidney dialysis I don't think that is very lucky. Do not trouble trouble until trouble troubles you. I am not a snarley garley old lady. Your mom is going to shoot you. You will go straight to hell for that. The dark grim reaper angels took her away at 65. Look how she used Maebelle. Everybody went to hell because of that gun. That was so evil. She should have gone to House of Horror/Wax. The bitch is back! You had better not touch a dick. These are the hands we're given. This is the land we live in - U.S.A. Freedom is not free. Move to Sweden, Switcherland, the Netherlands or Canada. You love Niagara Falls. You had better kick Free Will right in the balls. Hope, my nurse Scorpio practicioner got fired. You are a coward Mae. Where is your next meal coming from - COVID 19. Micah is in jail for a D.U.I. Job is your favorite. He did not curse God & die. That devil, satan, Lucifer, father of lies is cruel. Beware of, electronics, Lafassa, & King Kong - blueprints. God feels terrible what he did to you. You almost shot yourself because of that candy cane vibrator that Gracie Bathsheba gave you. Call upon the glorious white winged angel Michael. You are petrified of aides - look what happened to Freddie Mercury in Queen - Bohemian Rhapody. You are scared to death of Paul. What if your mother broke your jaw? You had better do every good deed that you can think of. You are a martyr & you've got the crown of righteousness. Lay it at Jesus's feet. I can do all things from Christ that strengthens me. Feed the ghost! Tell God a joke! Don't smoke!

You gave St. Peter a candle & he let you right into Heaven. You cannot stand that gay mother _____er Red Sea. He wants you to be a model & you are a brat. The drunks laid on top of your mother right in front of you. Red Sea was an actor pianist in New York City & he cannot drive, got put in jail when his mom died. Peace wants a cigarette. You are a whore. Whores make the best wives. You're being treated like a scapegoat. Don't ever tell me to _____ off! Venzuela was the prettiest girl in Zion Egypt High School & she o'd on Mother's Day. I cannot stand Gideon, her ex-husband. Who shot the Kennedy's? Venzuela believed in God! You had better know the difference between right & wrong.

Beware of blue fatal at the Humane Society. You want to choke that witchy bitch for firing you for getting too attached to the animals in on 8-10 1982. Scoot! Scoot! I can hear mom Loyal Dedication say.

Micah is on your slut list again. What the _____ is going on around here? You can casts spells! Your mom put you in jail. That young boy at the kidney dialysis center is awesome because he works for LIPS. I think God is awesome (A-absolutely - W-wonderful wizard - E-egotistical - S-stupendous - O-omnipotent - M-mesmerizing - E-eternal). They treat me like a queen goddess of the office. You can hear things & you can see things. Candle, candle, light on fire - tell me who to hire. My arm is sore from that COVID - A shot vaccine. I feel sorry for myself. Mom gave me no sympathy & called me poor pitiful pearl. Gay lesbian alcoholic Ecclesiastes is dead at 63 & she is a bitch. Look at all you did for her & she called you negative, negative, you have a big _____ing house what did she have. People are jealous of you, Mae. How bad did you hate Shop-a-Lot #666 #999 Agora, Mae? How bad did you hate cousin Pisces Faith that passed away at 65 from breast cancer.

You hurt God's feelings. The Holy Spirit is your favorite. Everything has been forgiven. Is there a hell? Cheer, my soul sister is dead & she is a bitch. All she wanted was that food stamp card. I've been thru diamonds. I've been thru minks. LOVE stinks. You are a witch, prayer warrior. TRANCES!

Wild, petite daisies are dancing around forked weeds. Stagnant heat is reflected from the cocrete earth Prairie grass with plum accents swings, while airy, beige moths touch their blades with staccato beat. Clover rooms with bug bitten stalks. Whipper snappers are courting to be plucked, & their heads of lacy pellets bombed forth by mischievous hands. Lavender faces & Queen Ann laces with bright sunflowers dipping their struggling lips to the quenching water. Along the banks, cockelberries wave to be. Snakes dive from intruders. Choruses of unseen insects harmonize with the living & the still.

Your mother said she loved your gay faggot brother but she did not like him. You had better put a nickel in between your spread legs. Pour me out a blessing. Feed the black cat Hershey's Licorice JuJu & the black & white cat Felix. Tangerine the orange cat is gone. My cat Thunder Theology Curiosity is not spayed & is the cutest tabby in the world. If my cat does not like you, we probably won't either. You almost lost your house Tara because of Hope, Micah, & Joy. I am mad & I want them dead. You are way too high to be driving my black panther Chevrolet AVEO that only had 26,000 miles on it & the lamp switch could have caught on fire. Now, I have a used car maroon wine Hyandei with 77,000 miles on it. It cost me $7,000. That salesman that died is a weasle.

You made a deal with God - no drunk driving. You cannot stand to have an arm put around you. Micah gives you the creeps. God said yes. Beware of Cancers - 4th of July is my favorite holiday, Valentine's Day. You are what you eat! Look at the shooting that happened in Las Vegas, Emminece. You cannot stand the name Lee Ann. You cannot stand to be slapped across the face. You had better not have sex in your mother's bed. You are being called CRAZY! You have no aunts or uncles. How many times have you been stripped? Why do black men want to go out with white women? God cannot stand violence. PEACE! I had a nightmare dream. Judas Iscariot from Camel Carrier Trucking Company is putting a needles apparatus in a baby girl's mouth who is crying & slams her mouth shut. I am scared she will swallow it & then I woke up.

Damn it to hell. Heart & soul is good lady down at Hebrew Tabernacle Episcopal Church passed away from cancer at 88. After I die, the books Jeans/genes, Agora, Crazy check & Queen Goddess of the office will live on. Who will get the royalties? Be careful! You may end up in my novel. Why are there so many diseases - pathology? All your friends are dying so young. What if your child O'd on codeine? This COVID-19 is getting on my nerves. Virgo Canaan is absolutely hilarious & is the right one for me. His good-looking brother says he is a narcissist & a psychopath. The 2 brothers do not get along. Canaan fixed me up free T.V. Emmanuel, a beautiful auburn haired, brown eyed girlfriend went to Zion, Egypt Community College together, smoked pot, drank beer, double-dated. I dated Eagle, a fat slob, but he was nice, fun. I liked him! We bowled, played cards, & went to a Fog Hat concert together. Some witch asked me to buy acid. I said no. Eagle was found dead shot in the head in a car on the side of the high-way. Eagle was dating a jealous cop's exwife. The cop got off & turned around & sued the city. We used to laugh at Welcome Back Kotter, give me drugs. Aaron, my best friend True/Trust/Truth who passed away at 42 years from a hougiens tumor, husband punched Eagle in the nose in a fair fight. Micah, my gay brother, loves eagles. Now is the beginning of the RESUMÉ. Emmanuel was a fellow Aquarius born on Valentine's Day like Cheer, my soul sister that passed away from an unknown disease, in a nursing home, & feeding tube. I am praying my ass off for Aaron's grandson 6 years old, that got attacked by 2 vicious Great Dane dogs, bit 11 times & a 100 stitches in his leg. Aaron & Forgiveness are my best friends. Sunshine & air is the balm for all ills.

Only scarred lives can really save. According to Jeanie Dixon, St. Peter represents Aries & is the greatest sign because he said Jesus was the son of God. John represents LEO. St. Jude, my favorite, represents Aquarius, & Judas Iscariot & Lazerus represent Pisces. Matthew, the tax collector represents Capricorn. Who likes tax collectors? God wants Mae to eat. I am on home kidney dialysis & this corona virus is getting on my nerves. Emmanuel's mother was very beautiful when she was younger. All Cheer wanted was my food stamp cards. Blessed has given up her 3 children to her mother. Her son is the good boy and he says I am good. Her older daughter has a smart mouth & her younger daughter is mean. I do not have a mean bone in my body. Pray for the children! Zion, Egypt is a wicked, evil town. Canaan never goes to church, is smart & Free Will is his best friend. Jesus is in the tribe of Judahs.

??? My wild German shepherd husky Calvin Klein. Oh, how I pray she got adopted. Beware of Virgo. Micah was a mean, mean little boy. Get out! Walk! All men want sex. Dr. Sweden at Our Lady of Mercy said I was afraid of sex & my mind races & gets off track. Feed the hungry! Mae spit on Faith's grave. Your mother is going to shoot you. I am petrified of guns & leukemia. Cain raped me in 1982 when I lived in brown town. I am killing all rapists! You had better get out that Bible & read it. An eye for an eye, a tooth for a tooth. Who killed my brother? You don't deserve to eat the crumbs under the Last Supper's table. Dr. Fabel thought he was possessed by the devil & shot himself - a good denist. Do you go to hell for suicide? You are a bride of the Lord, Mae.

The worse news I ever got was when Gift/gifted, a good Pisces guitarist, computer programmer at Camel Carrier Trucking Company passed away at 49. I am so jealous of Gift/gifted & want to talk to her. What happened?! I can hear mother Loyal Dedication, "Bully for you!" I would never say that to a child - positive reinforcement. She treated you like shit. Go live with your father, Perseverence. He did not give a hoot about us. How much child support did she get? You had better not drink or smoke when you are pregnant & you had better not shake that baby. Mom told you to pack all your clothes up & leave. You are so glad she is dead. Oh Lord, open my eyes to see what is beautiful. My mind to love what is good. My heart to know what is true. For Christ's sake. Amen. The mean bastard next door neighbor had better fix that fence. His wife has alheimers & is in a nursing home.

You are not born gay. It is a choice. That is my opinion. One of Micah's bi-sexual friend got shot, killed in the head for being with another lover. I liked him! That's when I was a picker at a clothing factory. That's when I had my collie husky, Tee, who was epileptic & I fed her phenobarbitol twice a day. She died in my arms when I had to put her asleep at 12 years old in 2006. I loved that dog! Do everything in your power to keep yourself alive. Don't worry! Be happy! If you do not take these kidney treatments you will die. Why is there a pandemic? You thanked God for another day. Micah is a tight wad; but he gave me $100.00 on my 63rd birthday 1-21-58. It was all Micah & Joy's fault you were hospitalized in Jebosite Haven at 50. They will pay. Vengeance is mine saith the Lord. Theo, my beloved cat is such a stinker poot! I miss volunteering at The Amazing Marines Soldiers of the cross. That place broke my heart. I got volunteer of the year & most knowledgeable in trivia. The trips were fun! The major was the funniest man alive & his beautiful wife was a saint. She got beat with the belt when she was younger. I do not believe in that! You are too sick & tired to beat a child with the belt or slap them. Godspell who I love slapped her son, Free Will, & went to bed & cried all day. Mae is very meek & weak. Call the squirrels Scamper. Rats with tails. I had a dream. Eternity, Mom's junkie nurse friend Japan's daughter whom I didn't like call me ugly. There was a man that looked like someone at Camel Carriers Trucking Company. Stop everything & write that com check for the broker. R732. Lucifer moved the company to the sunshine state. A mother whipped a bare baby's butt with card board. There was hard candy. I had a little boy & girl in my arms trying to find the lights. The children wanted to play poker. Pretty is as pretty does. It snowed today 2-1-21. I was switch board operator & money desk clerk, comdata liason for 17 glorious years. I liked that job! Throw that whisper screen out the window. Computers are taking over the world! Flattery will get you everywhere. God is whitey, with a long white beard & the true bluest eyes I ever saw. What color eyes did Jesus have? I have long blonde hair, gray blue eyes, 3 gold teeth, weigh 120 lbs. &

am not ugly. Say darn! Crap! King of the Jews got fired, resigned from Shop-a-Lot #666 #999. Shop-a-lot is an evil place. King of the Jews was co-manager & a snob. He knows where you live. H-A-L-O High altitude, low oxygen. Congratulations on your new book CRAZY CHECK! Who are you?

Follow that white gloved hand everywhere. You are psychic as hell. You are the branches we are the vines, you are reborn again per Nicodemis. He had a vasectomy. This weather is cruel & you had better not mess around with Mother Nature. I am a problem child. When I was cheerleader in Jr. High School, these mother _____ing niggers through a rock & cut my beautiful friend, Mediterranean Sea's head & blood was in my hand. I was so mad! Another friend got stabbed in the stomach. Two of the higher class negroes apologized for that. I loved those black people for that! That rock was intended for me. What if your child stole? I stole mice & bathing suits. Mom Loyal Dedication wants me to be strong & she is not fighting my battles for me. I cannot stand that lady Tested Curse. She talked about me like a dog said I wouldn't let my brother Micah in the house.

Mother Earth is weeping & Father time is sleeping. Micah has called me spacey 3 times. I hate him for that! This is what an awesome brother looks like. I was very popular in High School. What if your child o'd? The lithium shut down your kidneys. I have a catheder in my stomach. Godspell is under quarantine. She is the sweetest Capricorn in the world. Red Sea was gay & wanted to marry mother. They are both drunk & he lays on top of her right in front of me & calls me a brat. He was an actor & pianist in New York City & said he would sack groceries if mom would marry him. Everybody wanted to marry mother. Why? She was such an alcoholic bitch. Look at her mean facial expressions. Abel, Cain's brother was the funniest man alive dancing with a lamp shade on his head & exposing his big Virgo dick. I wanted to have his baby - Chassie Mae but True/Trust/Truth did not want me to have that baby. Circumsize that dick. Celibacy sucks! How many times have you been used? Mae loves mother nature. I killed every pedifile! You are being slapped across your face. How many lies have been told on you? God is afraid you will shoot yourself. You had better call upon the archangel Michael. I am so tired of being called stupid! Lorana Bobbitt is my hero. Look at the dick on that bug! The beautician swept under your feet & broke 2 mirrors - 14 years of bad luck. Cheer is eating chitlins & slaw penance.

Repent everyday. Mae has a heart of gold. Make new friends but keep the old. One is silver & the other's gold. You are a brownie. Be thrifty! Do you believe in reincarnation & dreams? I started working when I was 13 years old as a waitress at the Ideal Cafe for $1.00 an hour. My Aunt Wisdom & Uncle Humor owned it. If I made $5.00 in tips, I thought I was rich. Mother conficated all the money. Policemen got their coffee free. You had better say thank-you for that quarter tip & count that money back. Something is desperately wrong with that child. I was petrified of rain. The policeman peaches & the other policeman had lock jaw. Look at that mood ring. People are begging to go to New York at the concert Woodstock. You had better watch that purse. You were way too young to be working. You got all you wanted to eat for free. You are a martyr & humanitarian. Jesus does not eat ham because of the pig's feet. Wear black & white. I waitressed for 7 years. Trespasser/Transgressor owned a BBQ place. He had been to Our Lady of Mercy because of a divorce. He was a dirty old man & pulled out his huge dick & I poured sprite all over it. He fired me! Mom said that was okay. I loved my mom for that! I made potato salad, baked beans, slaw, & cut up riles, washed everything with vinegar & water, cleaned windows with bonomi. Tresspasser/Transgressor did not pay for his taxes. That is when a friend commited suicide.

It was all his fault I went to Our Lady of Mercy. His step-mother was a hoarder & her house was a mess. She lost 3 children. We went to the Bahamas together. The turquoise seas are my favorite. Micah & I played mastermind. You had better not eat bacon. How many times have you been abandoned? Mae almost stepped on a beautiful sting ray, caught 2 barracudas, & drank coconut goom bay smashes, went snorkeling. Let your hair blow back Daddy. The lightning is talking to you, got sea sick. That was the best fresh fish I ever tasted. It was Aunt Abundance's condemenimum apartment. I have been to the Bermuda Triangle twice. Remember the good times! You had better not go out with a black man.

It was a very expensive! Beware of the knive & beware of the full moon in Miami. People go there on their honeymoon. The Bahamas searched by bags looking for drugs. There was a black hole with no bottom & sharks surfed the floor of the ocean. Sand dollars, turkey wings shells, starfish are everywhere. Today is Sunday 9-6-2020. Thanks be to God. The Lord Jesus be with you. I had a crazy dream at 4 o'clock this morning sleeping on the couch after drinking a bottle of moscata wine & repenting. I was in this car with this young cute boy named Cody & we went to Shop-a-Lot. There was a swimming pool. The girl ran & dived in the pool. Cody was getting on my nerves. The fat bitch Gracie Bathsheba were fighting over the scanners.

I was buying all kinds of crap - rugs, clothes, sheets. There was this big fat white man with black Afro hair that called me an old lady. I said, "I resemble that remark." I love Jeremiah - the prophet. Why do you say peace when there is no peace? Peace was a beautiful art teacher & was agnostic. This is a beautiful sunshiney day after all the rain. Micah's birthday is 9-15 a Virgo. Keep on pluggin per Dad Perseverence & Peace. Swing low sweet chariot coming for to carry me home. Godspell cannot stand that black vice-principal for beating her son with a paddle & leaving bruises. You deserve every last penny of that social security. You had better thank God for another day. All you do is pray, because you are saved.

You are petrified of Stephen King's IT clowns. Oh, my God! When you die, is it a blessing' Angel I, Isabella, Jehosaphat, Ecclesiastes, Cheer, Sunshine, Messiah, Sarah Israel. Sing amen. Persistance is cussing God out during a lightning storm on a sand bar on Green River at Girl Scout Camp. Save a turtle. Inch by inch anything's a cinch. You will get kicked out of the Army for being gay or manic-depressive. It is your turn to get married. This is the land you live-in. These are the hands your given - the land of confusion. Pray for understanding. I lost my temper today with my cat, Theo. I feel so bad! You cannot stand pencil dicks. Penecostal dumped you & he was a mailman in Princeton stealing social security checks. I hate men!

Fornination & adultery is a sin.

Persistance LEO was your best friend. Is it suicide hour. Atlanta Rythym section - I may go as far a suicide tomorrow but I am not going to worry about it tonight. You are too scared to cry. My blood pressure is 88/72. I love Mother Teresa, the nun. You have got to quit smoking to get a kidney transplant. Pray hard! I have got to go to the laundry mat today & see my religious good Capricorn friend. I am off kidney treatment on Tuesdays & Saturdays. She cusses, too. Forgiveness, my best Scorpio friend curses like a sailor & got a job at Shop-a-Lot in the deli making $16.20 an hour. She lives in Owensboro where Johnny Depp was born, my favorite actor. Mery L Streep, Goldie Hawn, Bett Midler, Lucille Ball are my favorite actresses. Oh, an Bewitched Elizabeth Montgomery, Paul Lyrin, Frank Sinatra, Mia Farrow, Gregory Reck.

How many people have to die from this corona virus? You are treated like a queen goddess of the office. Lavender, purple, blue, pink are my favorite colors. You cannot take a bath & you cannot go swimming. You have to wash your hair in the sink. I feel sorry for myself. Poor pitiful pearl. You feel like you are paralyzed. Why did God make termites, roaches, fleas, ticks, spiders, snakes, wasps, hornets? You had better not tell Joy to get out of your house. She is so vain. You go insane when it rains. Why don't you get a generator? The demons are in your head. Your dead friends are alive & ressurected per Rev. Daniels. Your mother is going to knock the hell out of you. Your mother is mean, for shooting herself in front of you. That Catholic fortune teller is the prettiest girl you ever saw. There is an evil spirit following you around. You are higher than a kite!

If you snap me out of this, I will never do acid again. Theo, my tabby cat is my most precious child. Look what Hitler did to the jews. You are dutch & you had better go to

Sweden. Look what that black nigger did to that car salesman. He poured gasoline all over him & set him on fire. You had better get on those knees & say Lord have mercy. The devil made her do it! Look what happened to the children when you were on jury duty. They are sticking dicks in their mouths. This is a sick, sick world. What does this dream mean? You are with Malachi from Shop-a-Lot. You liked him. He was funny. We go to a large building delivering papers at 2:00 in the morning. You get clothes & you have not called your mother. She will be worried. I hope she has not called the state police. Holy ____! Do something Christian. There are people starving. Be of good cheer. I have overcomed the world.

Are you wiccan' witches get burned at the stake. God has heard every prayer. Pray for Haiti! People are doing meth. How many felonies did that girl at Amazing Marines Soldiers of the cross have? You had better beware of the black man from Cynthiana, a panther tatoo, & community service. You had better have faith as a mustard seed. Persistance who died is the most beautiful girl you have seen - a R.N. nurse. You had better watch that purse. You can get a D.U.I. driving on your medicine, a P.I. for walking on it. Remember that junkie Armaggedon who got killed by a drunk driver & you had better make sure those feet fit before you get married. He begged you for sex. I am not interested. Your mother said she was sorry he died. Mom was a great lady & Peace loved her.

Look how she used Maebelle. They went to Las Vegas, New York City, Arizona, Bahamas, Boston, York, Pennsylvania. God is a jerk! You are with Ms. God. You want the first woman president of the United States of America. You had better repent for that, Mae. It was all God's fault because of that 2009 ice storm - now look at COVID-19. God is killing people. Ms. God is loving, kind, compassionate, & merciful. Jesus forgave you everything! You miss your bewitching white cat with gold eyes, Wrangler. My halo is temporally out of order! I love God! I love Jesus! I love white angels. I love the Holy Spirit/Ghost but Wrangler I loved the most. He killed your cat! Shielded, yielded kill. You cannot stand Free Will. He is horny & he will use you. He is a fast talking salesman for stair lifts.

Get out of my house, Joy! The world is going to be destroyed. Beware of the red fox! Bob cats & fawns do not get along. How much did that floor cost to be replaced because of a leaking ice maker in the refrigerator? You are being sexually harassed & discriminated against. Whores, fornicators, homosexuals, sorcerors do not go to Heaven. The Bible contridicts itself in so many places. God is treating you like a queen goddess of the office. Look how many drinks your mother has had - the worst alcoholic you have ever seen & gay faggot brother Micah is just like her. Cousin Faith who died from breast cancer went straight to hell for that abortion & telling me to go to the food bank. Pisces & Aquarius do not get along. You wanted children. Mother did not want wild grandchildren. SHEETIE SNOTT. Everything will be alright.

Blood is running down Mary's leg. Peace, the great art teacher almost got killed in a car wreck. She was thrown out of the car & the truck driver lost his leg.

You are begging for mercy who died in a fire at Camel Carriers Trucking Company. Obedience, mean Jeanne's 17 year old beautiful daughter died in a car wreck, her step-son shot himself in the head on the side of the road, her other step son died of cirrhosis of the liver. They lost 3 children. Jeanne's house was a mess! I am not laughing! Micah likes graveyards. That is weird! He gives you the creeps! Do not touch me! Maebelle, red hair brown eyes rich bitch is smelling tasting that tea. Why is God mad at me? God is jealous & he is vicious. Men have enmity with God. Karma will get you, Mae. Poncho did a silkscreen of John Lennon the Beatle who got shot & commited suicide.

Mae is a helper & is going straight to Heaven. She has paid all her dues. Look what those hobos did. Apologize to God. You have carpotunnel from typing & writing. You get a crazy check. You love Biden! Micah is an alcoholic, got a degree in mixology & has bartended for 30 years at the Elks Lodge. He finally got a _____ing phone. You've got the sixth sense, mental telephathy. God knows exactly what you're thinking. God sees you naked. Pray your _____ off! God wants you to eat. Are dead people asleep? Jesus's hair is white. What color eyes does this good-looking man have? My drug buddy acid, mescaline, cocaine pot Fable passed away. She was Catholic & her father was a rich architect. Fable was my best friend in High School. You had better make a deal with God - no drunk driving. Idec hands are of the devil per Tree. Celebrate when you get reborn again. Jubilee!

Say a prayer for the damned. Hot damn! Dance & sing. I love the Pussycat Dolls! That black man tap dancing is the most talented man I have ever seen - The Wiz. I don't want to hear any bad news. Ease on down, ease on down the road! Trust in God's perfect timing. Joy has no patience whatsoever. You are too religious to get upset with God. How old is God? What is wrong with your hands? He is a great God! All your sins have been forgiven. You miss your 91 step mother, Laughter. Job, my favorite Taurus cousin who sold oxycotlen & got busted has a broken back, stroke & bad heart. He says you cannot be too young, too rich, or too skinny. His son Sodom was a lawyer & got busted for cocaine. The girl that Job thought was beautiful looked like a slut. Sodom got his shock probation & is remarried in North Carolina & doing well.

You have a statue of a girl holding a cat called Starsey Michelle Mystique, a naked lady statue called Queen Elizabeth, angels called Francesca, Chassie & Gabriel, Gardenia, a lucky Buddha. Rub a bob dub, thanks for the grub. Yeah, God! Charity is a bum. She is not so scared of anything! You had better fear God! Look what happened at Jurassic Park, Avatar, Deep in the Woods, The Greatest Showman, The Reverent, Black Mass, Public Enemies, A Star Is Born, Christopher Robin, Mary Poppins, The Book Club, The Butler, Mama Mia, Pirates of the Caribean, The Whales, Coal Miner's Daughter, Hope Springs, Meryl Streep & Johnny Depp are my favorites, Tommy Lee Jones was awesome in Abe Lincoln. Forrest Gump is getting made fun of - Sally Fields. Be patient! You wanted to get pregnant so badly. Marry a rich doctor & have 5 kids. Now, you are a barren old maid. That is the end of the world! Prophet got fired from Shop-a-Lot #666 #999 for health reasons. That is such a dirty company! His daughter got fired too from that witch prostitute Martha. Why did God make tornadoes, hurricanes? To kill people. Case closed. Abortion is murder & I had no idea what I was doing at 18. It was all cousin Faith's fault. The manic-depressive father of the baby Lazerus shot himself. I never told him. He did not go to hell. I prayed for his soul every night. We should have gotten married - a perfect couple. I paid dearly for that with 2 nervous breakdowns to Our Lady of Mercy 19-21. Door of Hope counselled me with Bible study. Forgiven & set free. Pray for your enemies. I love sweet tea for breakfast & the Penecostal driver for my kidney equipment. These masks are getting on my nerves. Pray for #5 Mae. Theo, my cat is choking. Holy, God, holy God hear my prayer. She is the sweetest child I have ever had. You had better not turn your back on God. Prayer is the wireless connection. Numerology & astrology is satanic. You are very superstitious. You are a prayer warrior. What does raped by the spirit mean? Penance. Do a good deed per soul sister Cheer. All of this sin was Eve's fault when she bit that apple because of the crafty serpent. Those cherib angels have already taken your raptured spirit to Heaven. All you have left is a body. You have a new spirit cloak.

Peacocks are beautiful birds. A bird's warble is more important than a stateman's speech. Suicide happens mostly in the spring. Why? You made a C in speech. Josiah, the red headed lawyer used the snot out of you. Sasha, witnesse's sister pulled a train & has a bubble brain, called 9-1-1 to bring her vodka & food & got put in jail. She has a beautiful blonde, green-eyed daughter. Her mother, weep, said she thought I shot mother playing poker. I have never touched a gun. She was Presbytarian & went straight to hell for that to be with mourn, the atheist. What if you had one green eye & one brown eye? They were good people. The lithium shut down your kidneys. You could have sued Joy, Micah, Hope, Dr. Trojan. How many times have you been sent up the river? God is dead is the evilest song I have ever heard by Black Sabbath. You want to fire Joy. Whoa black Betty bam da lamb. Black Betty had a child, the damn child went wild. WKTG - out to lunch with Aaron Bone. What the hell is going on around here? Oh, my God! Sprinkle, sprinkle fairy dust bitch cousin Faith. Your brown century bruick got stolen because you left the keys in it. Your mother Loyal Dedication came to the rescue. The purple rain drives you insane. Mae has been an absolute angel since God talked to you. Who is next? The police had better find your car. - joy riding. Your mother put a roof over your head & you & Micah are not ingrates. You had better do what Catholic priest Father Klon says - turn on the light. He is throwing a fit about Ms. Wieler's inheritance. Everything went to her boyfriend. God is treating you like a queen goddess of the office. Look what happened to Freddie Mercury.

Look what happened to Princess Diane. The only time mom apologized was when she called me a fat hog. I did not accept her apology! She had better fix the God _____ door! Jesus was a carpenter. Follow him around everywhere. You cannot watch The Omen. You cannot stand the name Damien. You are a lover not a fighter. It's not PMS, I am always bitchy. What if your father was a garbage collector. You are petrified of talented Gracie Bathsheba from Shop-a-Lot #666 #999. She was in foster care with a bone breaking disease in a wheelchair. Beware of Capricorn. I never thought I was better than anybody else. When your mother & father forsake you then I will lift you up. You are not a cold hearted bitch Mae. Your father was a Taurus on the cusp with Aries. You are an Aquarius sun, Aquarius moon, & Taurus Aries rising sign. My good Capricorn laundry mat friend is crying. Don't cry!

Where is beautiful French lady? She is almost 90 & the prettiest lady I have ever seen. Meri Ci Bogu, seph u pea. France passed away from cirrhosis of the liver at Camel Trucking Company years ago. She was a beautiful lady with red hair & brown eyes. She thawed a turkey in the dryer & her daughter cut off all her hair. I loved her! You come by it honestly. Honesty passed away. His sister had laser surgery & the doctor messed up & she died with 6 children. Zion, Egypt Hospital is getting sued. Slinedown - tell my mother, tell my father I have done the best I can - that this is my life. I hope they understand. I'm not angry. I'm just saved. Sometimes, you get by with a second chance. State of my head. I'll follow you down thru the eye of the storm. Don't worry I'll keep you warm. I'll follow you down as we travel thru space. I don't care if we fall out of grace. Micah is a greedy gut! Money talks. Bullshit walks. You have been called wicked. Moses, the deacon says you are not wickeds I loved Moses & Sarah Israel at the Hebrew Tabernacle Episcolpal Church. Sarah Israel died at 88. Moses is 92. May peace be with you, saint.

There are perverts in this dangerous hill billy drug town in the Bible belt. Canaan is the best looking single man you have ever seen. We do not always agree. Godspeed. I do not think gays are born that way. It is a choice. That is my opinion. That is an adbomination of the Lord. All you can do is love them. Pray before you faint. You crazy craven mortals better shape up or ship out down there on Earth. Everything I do, I do for God's sake.

Don't make me cry! Am I going to die? Not right now. Write this book, Queen Goddess of the Office first. I dreamed I broke a Pirante jar. I have seen pickle jars break & cut people's legs. Shop-a-Lot is a devil store. All they care about is the money.

I love Canaan! Cupid has got me now. I have one male boy doll named Zachary Oliver. Where is love? Does it fall from trees above? Is it underneath the willow tree that I've been dreaming of? Therapist Dr. Zack saved my life about my kidneys & was very good with children. I love children! Everybody is fighting over the book AGORA - fear of marketplace & crowds. Where lies the soul of Adam Lot? Charity is always broke & she makes $2000 a month $800 more than me. I always have to buy the food when we go out to eat. Sneezing makes me really, really mad. ____! These voices tell you what to do & put you down. I liked that female therapist - Jessie. You call the bank every day because of the scammers. Scammers are going to hell! Candle fire all aglow. Tell me what you know. Look what a saint Micah has been. Music is my junk now. God is love. It all ends in a confusing to laugh!

Shit, shower, & shave. Satanists are fools! Jebosite Haven was cruel.

How many times have you been reincarnated? How many past lives have you had. I am buying you a stairway to Heaven. You had better do everything Moses tells you to do. Mourn, atheist friend, & mom wanted you & red-headed lawyer Josiah to get married. There are crooked lawyers in Zion, Egypt. Wonderful Tahiti was a judge. Mom had friends in high places. Forgiveness, my best Scorpio girlfriend, that went to prison for 2 years for counterfeiting $20's & D.U.I.'s says Micah, my gay brother is a stupid queer faggot. She is so mad at Charity for wanting my stimulus check because I am not for Trump. Pray for America. I am petrified of clowns - IT. Oh, my God! People are eating shit! This is a sick, sick world. What if you get the corona virus? This year has sucked - 2020. Is it the end of the world?

The rapture - will you get left behind! You had better read John Jakes The Bastard, Irma Bombeck - If Life is a bowl of cherries than WHY AM I in the pits? Stephen King's books are evil. You have been sleepwalking & talking in tongues. God is great! God is good. Let us thank Him for this food. By His hands, we are fed. Let us thank Him for our daily bread. How bad does your mother hate you? Feed the ghost! Hope is a quack! The worst nurse practioner Dr. Sam in the shrinking business. She does not want to listen to your problems & is calling the EPO on you if you move. I hate that Scorpio bitch!

Mae wants to be rich & famous. My halo aura is temporarily out of order! You want to be an industrial psychologist. Phrenology reading bumps on the head. God is a jerk & I love Him more than anything! Jesus forgives everything!

You had better tell God a joke & make him laugh. Laughter is good medicine. What if St. Peter was holding the keys & standing by your bed? Give St. Peter a candle & he let you right into Heaven. What are they doing community service at the Amazing Marines Soldiers of the Cross? You are the boss! Micah is mean & destructive. You want Joy fired! You are a coward. All I hear from mom Loyal Dedication is you make me sick! Day is gone, from the lakes, hills, skies. All is well. Safely rest. God is high. May God give you strength when yours is gone. May His grace & mercy carry you on. May the unending love that He has for you revive your heart, & see you through.

If I was a virgin, I would be an Episcopal nun. Religion is witchery in the wrong hands. Mae is a prayer warrior raped by the spirit. What does that mean? God said thank you for your persistant candle-lighting faith, at the 50th class reunion, I did not drink a drop on Oct. 1, Alison's, sacred Jame's birthday. Something was wrong with the lights on my car & I hit a mailbox. The neighbors called the police cops. & a black cop came to my door & told me to put my German shepherd husky dog Calvin Klein up. I have night blindness & had to pay $100 for that mailbox - traveling mercies. I had a lousy time. Micah, my gay brother is going straight to hell for not praying. Your mother is a junkie. Armaggeden died from being hit by a drunk driver. You had better make sure the shoe fits. I have no desire to be with you. Scoot, scoot, your mother shot herself. You saw Alexis, the kindest, sweetest blind diabetic in your dream. We drank, ate, went to the Chippendales. Alexis - head operator at Camel Carriers Trucking Company. I am coming down to save you from poverty & hate. Ecclesiastes, gay lesbian alcoholic cusses, can't walk, falls, & won't eat. All she does is drink beer & is grumpy saying I have a big _____ing house, what does she have? I have problems of my own. She says you are negative. Fasting & prayer gets out demons. Think positive. I keep losing my gray bomb car in my dreams. A kitten is in my purse. Your mother is a devil worshipper. They are people, too. You are so sick at your stomach & 911 is not just another day. You had better not call somebody a fool. All fools in the pool! You had better not have sex in her bed. You had better not tell me to __ off! Do not tread on me. Mae cannot stand that Dr. Trojan at Jebosite Haven. You are 50 AARP golden year sucked! I am thru sucking dicks. Look at that blue moon. You are so bitter. Your mother is a bitch. She used rich bitch Maebelle & treated you like a scapegoat when she was dying from throat cancer at 65. I know Jack SH#T! Watch it bleed! I can't stand the color red-courage. You had better run from the devil, a vain bastard. How many angels have fallen out of the skies? Pray your __ off! Your mother does not believe a word you say. How many times have you been raped? You threw those keys at her. She was only

21

trying to help you. Comet is your password as liason with comdata. You cannot stand that female vice-president, Hate, & you cannot stand the presidents Herod & Lucifer. Mae has been thru hell! Why is pee yellow? You've got a benign tumor in your neck. Job is your favorite cousin & he is your god father. Look at all the devastation. Leave the tumor alone. How much did that cost? God is not dead. This medicine makes you sleepy. You are drowning & you had better mind your own business. Jesus is coming like a thief in the night, riding a white horse, wearing sandals. Why do we have to die? Mammy does not know the answer to that question. Her sister committed suicide. Mae, where did you get that manic-depressive, bi-polar, schizophrenic gene? Robin Williams hung himself. That is the saddest thing I have ever heard. A Star is Born with Lady Gaga was a sad, sad movie. You are groovy. What if Lazerus's baby was premature? Name that baby July Seven. You had better stop those contractions. Is this real or is this folklore? Om made pod may hum. You are so dumb what if the child was retarded? The funniest thing I ever heard. I sat up in my bed talking in my sleep. Tobacco is nivero - some nonsense word. Mother said who are you? I said Kelloggs cornflakes. She said go pour yourself back in a bowl. When she was dying, she said guess what, chicken snot. I'll never love again. God works in mysterious ways. What is Lady Gaga's real name? Pauline's house of prostitution. Getting fired from Shop-a-Lot #666 #999 was a blessing in disguise because of my kidneys. Fight depression like a plague. I cheered & worked at Ponderosa when I was in high school. That's when my cousin Faith yanked me up & got me an abortion from Lazerus's baby. I was barely 18 10 weeks along. I had a black & white rabbit & Mom told me to get that _____ing rabbit out of the house. I drove a blue lumina 500 bomb & I liked that job. I got a better job working in a factory at York. The manager was so good-looking & I quit like a fool to go into nursing school. If you go in a church with the cross upside down, you had better get out! I loved that job! Air gun, fiberglass, stenciling boxes was right up my alley. I had a nervous breakdown at 19 because I thought I was a murderer and another one at 21. When Lazarus shot himself, I felt like it was my fault & went to Our Lady of Mercy & I slit my wrist with a razor because I wanted to be with monk. He was only 23 years old. I will never have another abortion. Monk is in heaven in a half-way house for suicides reading the Bible. I will be with him one day. I never told him I aborted his child & prayed his soul out of hell. In Zion, Egypt Community College, I worked in the media center library 10 hours a week putting up books, typing, folding magazines, & filing. I liked this job. In the library, I would check out some really cool art books & classics. I made 3 C's in college - Sociology, English 102 & Speech. I had a 3.6 g.p.a. I loved school & graduated in 1981 with 2 degrees - Associate in Arts (all the prerequisites to R.N. Nursing) & Associate in Applied Science (secretarial administration). I quit taking the 1500 milligrams of Melaril & everything clicked. I did not think I was smart. That was a good year. Wear royal blue for psychic awareness. Why are you scared of everything? I am not scared of living. I am just scared of dying - Kubler Ross. I am 99% art. Theo is the most precious child cat I have ever had; but, she poops & pees on the rug by the bed. Why? The cookie lady passed away down at the church. She was a good old lady. Dearest beloved. God giveth & the Lord takest away. You thought Taurus Rev. Elisabeth was the best priest. Lay hands on me. Look what happened to Jonah & the whale, the prostitutes & the cake in Hawaii, the big black man that helped her when she fell & spilled all her money, her cat P.K. - preacher's kitty. Put me back on that prayer list. Blessed are the poor. Say a prayer for the damned. Another friend bites the dust. She was pretty, talented & successful - a whore clean for 34 years. 62 yrs. old. What a bitch born on 12-5-58. What did she die from? She took ballet, an old high school crony. Did she __ niggers for pain pills? Was she rude? Peace be with you - R.I.P. Go shout it on the mountain! Jesus Christ is Lord! She looked like a Hollywood famous star celebrity. Your body goes to medcure body to science. They will pay for everything! Thank God for another day. Who the _____ knows & who the _____ cares. I do! You had better be reborn again - Nicodemas al Shop-a-Lot #666 #999. Nicodemas thought I was pretty, wanted to live with me, smoked, had a vasectomy, took good care of his mother, looked old, & bought me chocolate covered cherries. I am so sorry. I am not interested. You do not turn me on like Canaan does. Look what the doctor did to your nose. I do not think I am pretty! I think I look like shit! I was so beautiful when I was younger. It's a bitch to get old & ugly. Wisdom comes with old age. Hind sight is better than fore sight. I am old but I'm not dead. God blessed me with another day. I had a dream about Sarah Israel, Moses & India. I was cleaning a room. Dead people are trying to tell me something. I had a new house in my dream with a dog & it was full of people I did not know. What if there is a nuclear war? How many wars do we have to go thru to get to the promised land. Camels cost $4,000. Return to Bethlehem. Your favorite apostles, disciples are Simon & Andrew, prophets Job & Jeremiah. Why does God hate me? God does not hate people. He loves everybody! You are with peace, the great art teacher - Aries 4-3. The prettiest lady who ever was agnostic & died at 89. She was your Mom's best friend! You had better not talk to strangers. You almost commited suicide because of a candy cane vibrator that that fat bitch Grace Bathseba gave you at Christmas at shop-a-Lot #666 #999. Michael, the arch angel saved you. How can you believe that there is no God? Look how many poisonous snakes are in Australia, my aunt on Dad's side. Esther, her beautiful daughter has skin cancer, rides horses, is a principal of a school. Is she a bitch? The world is white. The world is black. You cannot stand the name Alice in Wonderland. Eat me. Look what happened in the animal house. Who is John Belushi? It is Judgement day. You had better not raise that voice at your favorite Aunt Beautiful Patience - a Scorpio. Uncle Protection loved her! You are just like this aunt. Your mother is too rough & too tough. Cleanliness is next to Godliness. You have absolutely no respect for your mother. Look what happened to Forgiveness's mother at Our Lady of Mercy. The mean nurses & doctors gave her shock treatment 23 times. You are going to die in a car wreck - $100,000. You had better pack everything & leave. Beware of Taurus! Your mother went straight to hell for shooting herself. You had better bless thy food. Your name is in the book of names. Cousin Faith is a murderer. Aunt Abundance got married for money. You cannot stand her husband. He was a millionaire & ate every one of those corn chips, twiddling his thumbs on how to make more money. You cried when your mother died. Mae is a slut! I am not a greedy gut! Go live with your father, Perseverance. God cannot stand Joy, your best friend, that locked you up. You had better not get drunk. You cannot stand Trump. I know God! Mae went straight up in the rapture. You did not get left-behind. The college had dances & I used to date blonde hair blue-eyed Jordan who is very religious now. Jordan did cocaine & he was the one I should have married. Suck my pud. That is such a jerk! Canaan cannot stand Jordan (Thaddeus). Calm - not speed. God's creation is so beautiful! I worked at the Travel Lodge for my Aunt Wisdom & Uncle Humor as a waitress. The new proprietor fired me for doing drugs. I hate that man! Nobody likes you. Everybody hates you! Go outside & eat worms. I love Micah! It is time for my home kidney dialysis treatment. You have got to stay alive. I worked at Mom's Real Estate office as receptionist & cleaned 3 offices. Mom was the best bitchy boss. I answered the phone, typed letters, wrote ads, took pictures of houses, filed. That is when my brown Century Buick got stolen because I left the keys in the car. Somebody went joy riding & ran out of gas on the highway. My car was returned. I loved Mr. Roach that cussed out a policeman, Mr. Star who stole a car, a man named Skinner that was a drug dealer, a black haired beauty that could not stand wind, a beautiful girl who tried to teach me how to drive a stick shift, the owner & developer who made B's in business school. One of the realtors got fired for slapping a man who called her a liar. I worked there for about 4 years making minimum wage while going to school. I did not like Tested Curse. My brother & I have streets named after us. I am not a snarley, garley old lady, a devil or a fat hog. Mae is a reincarnated Mary Magdeline. Life's a bitch & then you die. I am so tired of being used by men. I have been puking my guts up. I couldn't keep down water. My right wrist hurts. I think I have carpotunnel. I have a catheder in my stomach. Where is my love, Theology my cat? When your mother & father forsake you, then I will lift you up. People are calling you crazy. The lawn man of Tara abode is a good, big black man - Methodist. The next door neighbor's snorting turned me off! He is a gourmet cook. Be nice to him. Charity & I are not getting along after all the deaths at Shop-a-Lot #666 #999 - Angel I, Isabella, Ecclesiastes, Cheer, Jehosaphat, deformed T.R., Sunshine. I cannot stand to be called LEE LEE, which means meadow dweller, gray, physician. Love your enemies. God is on your side. Your mother will stab you with a fork if you fart at the dinner table. Why is everything green - money, fertility. Mae followed God's white gloved hand around everywhere. You are reborn. I tore the nail off my left toe & it bled like a stuck pig. I poured peroxide on it & watched it bubble, fizz. 2-7-21 It snowed & the cruel winter weather is frigid frezato 23° on Sunday. I wish I could have sex with Canaan & it would not hurt like a bitch, "but, with this catheder in my stomach would that be virtually impossible. Hershey Kiss Licorice Juju, the outside black cat that I feed & water is limping. There is another big black & white cat named Felix. Tangerine, the orange cat, disappeared. I love my sweet indoor, unspayed tabby cat, Theo! Death is not a blessing. Death is cold. Death is cruel. Death is mean. Death is sad. That is my opinion. There are dark spiritual wars - carry a sword. I AM THAT I AM. God is kind. What is wrong with your mind? You are kin to the sleeping prophet Edgar Cayce by marriage. You had better not commit adultery with the heating, cooling electrician Benjamin Zebidiah. He is a Virgo 9-1, and he did not repent. Micah is putting on a big fascade. Micah, my gay faggot brother got $21,000 from me when mom passed away & said if I hadn't given him that money that would be the end of us. I was exexitrice & I did all the work in 1994.

Seek & you will find. Ask & you will receive. Knock & the door will be opened. When 2 or 3 are gathered together in prayer, Jesus is in the midst of them. Do not bear false witness against your neighbor. You had better not take the mark of the beast. #666 you will go straight to hell for being gay & atheist & you had better not say God ___. The Holy Spirit/Ghost has a personality & you should always praise God. Pedifiles are going straight to hell! That little son-of-a-bitch had better not call you per mom. You had better not pick anyone else in that 2005 black Aveo panther. You have cancer insurance. I know what it's like to be poor. The poor in spirit will see God. The beatitudes are my favorite - Mark V. Peroxide gets out blood. Hairspray gets out ink. Why did God make maggots? Your head is getting big because you wrote 3 books on Amazon.com - Jeans/genes, AGORA, crazy check. Queen Goddess of the office is your 4th & last novel, book. God treats you like a queen goddess. Please read all of them & enjoy. Jubilee! Allejulah!

God has blessed you so much! Why is there so much pain & suffering? Pray to St. Jude, one of my favorite disciples, apostles. You are so proud to be an Aquarius 1-21-58. They are very eccentric! How many crowns do you have - the crown of righteous. Place it at Jesus's holy feet. Joni Ereckson Tada is a goody goody 2 shoes, paralyzed from the neck down, religious, good artist with teeth, got married & I love her books. French lady from the Amazing Marines Soldiers of the Cross is the most beautiful older 88 year old lady I have ever seen just like my beautiful step mother laughter that died when she was 91. She thought nose diamonds made you look like a whore. My nose diamond fell out twice. I give up! Jesus is a Nazarene in the tribe of Judah. Canaan tells me all kinds of secret tales about people. You had better not mess with Mother Nature. That black man at the delapidated laundry mat gave you a B+ in looks. I love that black man! That wild child boy Christopher was my favorite. We used to play games, eat popcorn, & watch T.V. television together bonding. St. Christopher was a good saint. He protected the innocent children. Kittens grow up to be cats. Turn the other cheek. Tommy Lee Jones, Meryl Streep, Johnny Depp, Dustin Hoffman, Gregory Peck, Doris Day, Goldie Hawn, Bette Midler are the most awesome actors. I ever saw. Elizabeth Taylor, Gildna Radner, Chevy Chase, Church lady, Jane Curtain, John Belushi, Bill Cosby, Denzil Washington, Ed McMann - here's Johnny. Talk to the marijuana plant. I did acid (L.S.D.), mescaline, cocaine, PCP (horse tranquilizer), valium, speed. I was a horrible drug addict. God's hand touched me when I was 26 & my appendix exploded & I almost died of peritonitis. Micah's appendix burst too when he was 35 right after Mom died. I took care of him & prayed my ass off for him. Micah tore up the stereo & the screw in the stove. You whoosh, come down here & fix this stereo. He jumped all 5 stairs after me. Okay, it's time for you to go, leave. Aunt Abundance & Messiah, gay organist at Hebrew Tabernacle Episcopal Church were still alive. Now, they are gone. Is gay brother Micah saved? I saw the praying hands on a winnebago wheel in the hospital parking lot at night. Okay, God, I'll keep praying. What did your Dad mining engineer professor at U.K., captain in the Marines Taurus do? Absolutely nothing. Feed the ghost! Micah is a sissy. He'll hit a woman but he won't hit a man. Why does God not like black people? He put pubic hair on their heads. Your grandmother, Mammy, says you had better not go out with a black man. I do everything my beloved grandmother tells me to do. You had better pray for Discernment, your grandfather you never knew. Shoot the ghost! Call the police! Look what that cop did to that black man. He killed him. That is bullshit! O Lamb of God that taketh away the sins of the world. Have mercy upon us. Oh Lamb of God that taketh away the sins of the world, grant us thy peace. Your mother put a roof over your head & she died in Tara adobe abode. Get out of my house, cousin Faith who died of breast cancer at 65, aborted my child, & told me to go to the food bank. She went straight to hell for that! I am the one who got punished. Count your blessings is the only nice thing your mother ever said. Lazerus, the father of the baby, commited suicide shot himself in the head. Faith got to have her 5 kids. They are good children. Leviticus is my favorite, her son. His father, Genesis, was mayor & sold his soul. God restoreth your soul. We are having Christmas parties - strimp, tenderloin, wine & rum punch. Regrets only! Remember the good times! Who crashed this party?! Wear green skirt, maroon & white sweater, maroon hose. We were not rich! You are staring at that candle. What if St. Peter was by your bed? You would shit! That was the most pitifullest sight I ever saw when Mom was crying because U.C. (Ugly Cat) was dying. U.C., what does it feel like to die? She answered soft & fluffy. U.C. went into remission of cancer for 5 years. She used to bring us presents - shrews, rabbits, garter snakes. We had this precious cat for 9 years. - 7th Heaven - I dreamed I was on a bus & we soared thru the sky. The first place was the animals. I did not question why.

Nobody has a clue when Jesus is coming back. Your body is your temple. Do not destroy it with drugs, alcohol, foul language, incest. Don't ever call someone a fool! All fools in the pool! I know jack SH#T! You were on swim team, got 1st place in backstroke, 3rd place in freestyle, learned how to save lives in the lake at Girl Scout camp, could do flips, dives off the board, swam 2 miles a day, made a 95 on the swimming test, & canoed the Green River, White River, & Lake Malone. You were a good swimmer - breast stroke. Now, with a catheder in your stomach for home kidney dialysis, you cannot swim, bathe in the tub anymore because of infection. Woe is me! Mark Spitz is my hero! The Guardian was a good movie. Shop with a cop! When I did drugs, we called cops pigs. It is so dangerous to be a narc! Darwin's theory - did we evolve from apes? Love the busy life. What if there is a fire & I am hooked-up to the cycler machine. I am so deathly scared of fire. Forgiveness's parents house burned down to the ground.

I had a friend that was chopped-up in little bity pieces when they were on drugs. That's been a long time ago. My left toe is raw where I peeled, picked the toenail off. You know what it is like to be poor as dirt. Happiness is more important. In Chinese astrology, you are a dog & in the house of friendship. Every hair on that head is counted. Heaven is my home. That is where all my deceased friends are. Bewitched, Johnny Quest, Sunshine, Blossom were my favorite shows. You've got the 6th sense, Mae.- the shining. Red rum - murder spelled backwards, all work & no play make Jack a dull boy, here's Johnny! I loved Aaron & True/Trust/Truth, my best Scorpio girlfriend that passed away from a hockien's tumor. We will meet again on a concert on cloud nine. She was only 42 & I cried my eyes out! The grim reaper is out to get good people. Cheer, Persistance, Gift/gifted were the closest sisters. They are pretty, alive, & resurrected & they are trying to tell you something from the spirit world. You had better not whistle passing a graveyard. Bless their hearts! This is wicked freezing, frigid weather! Casper is a friendly ghost. You had better not flip out! You had better pull those boot straps up & go on. You had better not spank my child. Save yourself! Look what girls gone wild are doing. Ecclesiastes deceased gay lesbian alcoholic will get her revenge. She's going after Joy & Happiness. You watched her beat Joy up. You had better stand up for yourself. You saw an elf! You are not in good health. Hope, nurse practitioner is a quack - a mean Scorpio. You had better watch your back. Shop-a-Lot #666 #999 told all kinds of lies on you - you burn down the hospital, strung up black people. You don't even believe in slavery - KKK Ku Klux Klan. Look what they did to black people, niggars.

King Baol is the rudest, crudest black man & said they would take up a collection of money to pay for your medicine. He is going to choke you & he did not like you. Was Jesus a black man? No. Where lies the soul of Adam Lot? You are smoking pot - a hallucigenic. Low & behold, I AM an angel. Your troubles will be laid low & next time drink water not Swedish absolute. Her navy calico dress was beautiful & I could not see her face. You had better get mase. What if you got raped & had a black baby? He is in prison for 7 years for robbing a bank. Take that clonopine. The Amazing Marines Soldiers of the Cross are calling you crazy. The girl turned herself into the police for doing meth. You made an F in Spanish - CACA! Beware of the mon mon man up at Jebosite Haven. God has many disguizes & size of the penis matters. I cannot stand pencil dicks!

What if you had a dick, Mae? All men want is sex & blow jobs. Charity said she did not use me; but, I have to pay for dinner every time we go out. Who would have the balls to ask for your stimulus check because I am not for Trump. You have been mentally & emotionally abused & are tired of being called fat & stupid. When I worked at the Real Estate office, there was a nice lady that had a retarded son. The neighbor on the street behind my house, was throwing a fit about black people buying the Islam house. All I did was listen. Black people have moved in the $200,000 house across the street. Are they uppidy niggers? Why does God hate me? God does not hate people - He is pure LOVE. Mae has been tested way too hard!

Joy wants to slit a wild hogs throat. I am scared of wild hogs with tusks. I cannot shoot a gun & I can not use a knife to kill anything compassion, my best Sagittarius girlfriend that died from lung cancer is in Heaven. We took good care of her. Will she come back & haunt that old trailor? Her crazy ex-husband is not allowed in my house. Tara abode. I loved Ruthie! 52 years old! Will she come back for me? Take me to the other side. Ghosts are everywhere! You had better pray & you had better be saved. HO-LEE-CHIT! Who called the sheriff? Who are you God?! You are wicked, Mae. Beloved Moses 92 year old deacon at Hebrew Tabernacle Episcopalian Church says you are NOT wicked. God is my gun! You are paranoid as shit! 9-1-1 is not just another day. Pray for America! Kidney dialysis is the hardest thing you have ever done. You have been an absolute angel since God has talked to you. You are Catholic as hell! Love casteth out all fear. Pray for more love. Cousin Faith went straight to hell for aborting your baby. That is murder. Sprinkle, sprinkle fairy bitch!

Faith without good works is dead. 3 men died & are at St. Peter's Heaven's gate. St. Peter tells them you have to have an appropriate gift to get into Heaven. The first man said candles. St. Peter said you can come in. The 2nd man had keys & said they were bells. St. Peter said you can come in. The 3rd man had a pair of women's panties, underwear. St. Peter raised his eyebrows. The 3rd man said they're Carols. I would freak if St. Peter was by my bed. Forgiveness, my best Scorpio girlfriend, is going to cuss him out if St. Peter doesn't let her thru those pearly gates. Amazon keeps calling & saying they are going to debit $799 from my account for an order I did not place. Is this a scam? Scammers are going to hell! Satan is spreading his wings & laughing. How many shootings have there been? You cannot go swimming with a catheder in your stomach. This corona virus & home kidney dialysis is getting on your nerves. Jesus is not a black man. You had better read the Koran. Indians are very beautiful. Aunt Beautiful Patience Scorpio was so gentle, kind - my favorite aunt. Do everything she says to do - tornado, twister. Go outside & get your cat, Wrangler, white cat with gold eyes. That tornado sounded just like a train 2 blocks from my house. I was so glad to see brother Micah! Lord have mercy! The tornado was in November. Messiah, gay organist, who passed away at 80 wants to know why did God make these _____ing things. He was such a good man! Do not have sex in your mother's bed. You cannot go to Corpus Christi Texas because of your pierced ears. I am so jealous of guitarist Gift/gifted who died at 49, 30 years computer programmer, cat rescue, green peace at Camel Carrier Trucking Co. She was a good Pisces hippy & I want to talk to her. What happened? You had better say love you, good-bye. How dare you call your mother a bitch! Go live with your father is you blasphemy or drink before your 21. Your parents went thru a horrible divorce. Mammy, my beloved grandmother cannot get those earrings out of my ears. She cannot stand that drug addict R.N. Nurse, Japan. I was 13 when she died. My whole world crashed. She is glad to see you, wiggle worm. Give her a hug! Do not provoke your children to wrath! Angels are answering distressful calls just as fast as they can - godspeed. The purple rain drives me insane. You take nut pills, Mae. Mourn, the atheist & Mom Loyal Dedication are making fun of Jesus. God is going to treat you like a queen goddess of the office when you go to Heaven. Jesus was cruelly treated & died on that Calvary cross for our sins.

Is the anti-Christ, beast, diablo, satan, Lucifer here on this Earth? Read Revelations. Do not turn your back on God! This world is going crazy - Crazy Check. You had better not cuss God out like I did. He forgave you! God is forgiveness. Lordioso. There are tumors with teeth. One of your friends at Camel Carriers died from an inoperable brain tumor. I loved him! Do you hear & see things? You cannot buy LOVE. I loved Paul, the con artist, that passed away from aides, stroke. He was a musical genius who played the piano. Lazerus - what a talented guy. Do as I say not as I do. These Trump supporters are crazy! Biden all the way! You are going to shoot yourself because of this weather - ice. Don't do that Mae, your insurance policies won't be any good. A rich person getting into Heaven is like a camel going thru an eye of a needle. I am very poor. Nostradamas was a famous prophet. He prophesized Hitler, the evil man who killed the jews. You want to argue today? 2-11-21 Look at all this _____ing shit! Why is winter so cruel? Shop-a-Lot #666 #999 only cared about the money, I did not get my unemployment, & I was treated like shit for 10 years. It was all kindness's & Gracie Bathsheba's fault, they are control freaks. I expect to get paid for these books - Jeans/genes, AGORA, crazy check, Queen Goddess of the Office. You are taking too long God. I am running out of time & patience. Sit tight! I AM coming down to save you from poverty & hate. Who is writing this book? You are. Who saved the world? You did. Every name is important in the Book of Lambs. Ice skating, swimming, diving, gymnastics, cheerleading, basketball are my favorite spectator sports.

Religious cults are drinking cianide & dying, killing themselves, they are handling poisonous snakes. Am I wiccan - prayer witch? Weebles wobble but they don't fall down. No, I am Catholic, crazy Episcopalian. Mom said I was a martyr. The word was made flesh. God is the same yesterday, today, & tomorrow. Feed the ghost! You are a bride of the Lord. Cheer says penance - do a good, kind deed to make up for all the bad you have done. Sadducee has 6 kids she doesn't take care of. Disobedience, her father, drank himself to death & died at 40. He was the best looking man I have ever seen. You had better not flip out! God cannot stand drugs. Aaron's 6 year old grandson that got chewed up by 2 vicious Great Danes with a 100 stitches in his leg. Lord have mercy who died in a fire & her son accidently shot himself. Do something Christian. Take her to your shrink & buy her catfish. You have fallen out of grace, Mae you are dying & you get blessed for writing a book. Companion is a mean McCoy. Bless the poor. Jesus is coming back to judge the living & the dead.

God said yes to your deal - no drunk driving. You cannot stand that Judge Wonderful Tahiti. He got you out of jail. You are cursing Persistance out. Your mother & brother are very mean to you - get out of the car. They took the mark of the beast. Your mother cannot stand grease call the law to come shoot this ghost! He loves me, he loves me not. First comes love, then comes marriage, then comes a lady pushing a baby carriage. You are hearing dead people. Godspeed. Why did God make black widows? You have so many questions. You are brown nosing God. You are very thorough & efficient. Mae has been treated just like a criminal; but, has commited no crime. You had better not croak. I could have had a good job at the hospital; but, Mom wanted me to stay at the Real Estate office. I got a job as a receptionist at a milk company & they laid me off. Then in 1982 I got a job at the Humane Society & got fired for getting too attached to the animals & got put on unemployment. I wanted to choke that witchy bitch! Then I got a job at Buckles N' Belts when I lived in brown town. This morning 2-12-21, I had a dream I had 2 cute boys - Laken Forrestor & Matthew Conner. I want 3 more children - Elijah Christensen, Jesse Aaron, & Fawn Mariel. I am a good Mom. Black Betty had a child, the damn thing went wild. Bam da lamb. I am 63 & cannot have children - maybe in my 2nd life. Manic-depressives cannot adopt. Sweet, religious Door of Hope counselor Scorpio lady prayed for me about my terrible abortion of shot in the head Lazerus that cousin Faith aborted - Alison Rain, Joshua (to kill) Alex. I wanted children so badly! Now, my beloved pets, animals are my children. - Theo, my cat.

Women do it for LOVE. Men do it for pleasure. Be of good cheer I have overcomed the world. Children are very expensive - diapers, food, clothing, WIC, medicine, day care, cars, college, but they are worth it. It is going to be a sad day when I die. Amen - so be it. Sprinkle, sprinkle fairy dust Faith bitch! Our Lady of Mercy twice because of that 19-21. You cannot stand Pisces. Beware of LEO's - opposite heart sign of Aquarius. You are the favorite - Lee Lamb. God is LOVE. You can see things & you can hear things. It is a gift! Say a prayer for the damned. Follow God's white gloved hand everywhere! Beware of Taurus. You are on a mission. I got put in jail twice - once for a D.U.I. that was dropped & once for incarceration court order to House of Horrors/Wax. I lost that job. Then when I got out, I got a job at a nursing home & that big bitch said quit or be fired. I quit & went to a fast food restaurant, Burger King which I hated.

I got a job at Camel Carriers Trucking Company as switchboard operator & money desk liason to Com Data. I loved that job for 17 years. We played hard & we worked hard. The company moved to Florida. I went to Car-Hart as picker & quit. Then I got a job at Shop-a-Lot #666 #999. I got fired for solicitating my book Jeans/genes. I hated being cashier. I only liked people greeting. There are fake Christians, false prophets, end of the world times. All my friends are dying. Pray for good luck. Rub Buddha's belly. Buddha was an old man at Mom's real estate office. He was my favorite. I used to rub his bald head & he would say he was meaner than a red bottom spider. Mom was hanging out with a bunch of gay people & drank & smoked herself to death. I love Doral cigarettes. Your mother got her feelings hurt when you called her a bitch. I saw Godspell on acid. Mother did not want grandchildren because Micah & I was so wild. She got her wish. You told your mother __ you! in a dream because she was selling the house. You've got your precious child cat Theology to take care of. Then, you can't find your car at the mall. The kidney people have been so kind to you. You thanked God every day for that financial waivor. You only get $1200 on social security. Charity gets $2000. Life is not fair. All cheer, soul sister, wanted was that food stamp card. I expect to get money for Jeans/genes, AGORA, crazy check, queen Goddess of the Office. Why is there so much pain & suffering? Why are there flesh eating bugs? Why are we not considered a part of the family? Your fat bitch cousin, Leah, who is in Crusade for Christ. My aura is magenta. Heaven is for real & God loves the children. The whole ___ed up world has to wear protective masks because of the corona virus. Gracie Bathsheba was a holy terror in that wheelchair & sued Shop-a-Lot for her gangreen cut arm. She is now on disability. Gracie Bathsheba talked about people like dogs. She is a Capricorn, sheep in wolves clothing, huge Atilla the Hun. When she's not happy, nobody's happy. You could have sued Shop-a-Lot for the lies they told on

31

you - you burned down the hospital, you strung up black people. You don't even believe in slavery. You had better pray to stay alive. Your best friend cheer was black. This world is mean. You are petrified of black hair.

God cursed the negroes. Canaan's sweet, good-looking brother artist wants to dance. He says his brother Canaan is a narsissist & psychopath. Your mother is telling you to stick the house up your ass. Read the Koran. Look what the doctor did to your nose. You want to sue his ass! We are doomed! You cannot stand the name June. God said He was sorry He scared you. I had a friend that was on drugs & chopped up in little bity pieces. Dr. Fable thought he was possessed by the devil & shot himself. Mother Loyal Dedication shot herself. Monk Lazerus shot himself. Andrew shot himself. I have been thru 8 suicides. That is evil! There are evil spirits. You had better do everything Moses tells you to do. You will go straight to hell for commiting suicide. Sticks & stones may break my bones but words will never hurt me. Is there a lake of fire? I cannot watch. Do not touch me!

Your father, Dad, did not give a hoot about you - Perseverence. Look what that policeman did to that black man - bull SH#T! Charity is the luckiest person in the whole world! Her manic-depressive bi-polar daughter & son-in-law bought her a new water heater. My water heater cost me $900 & had to be inspected on my credit card. I have had no one to help me. Forgiveness, my best friend, put her 2 14 & 17 year old granddaughters on birth control. That is very smart. I talked to Canaan. He is very intelligent & I learn a lot about politics. He thinks I am a dumb, mean girl - that hurt my feelings. I have a very simple life. Simplicity is the keynote & pride bars the way. You had better be careful what you wish for. I want that star, I want it now & I don't care how. You just might get it. You may regret it!

The scariest whipping I ever got was with the belt. There is no way I could beat a child with a belt or slap them. That is child abuse. Why would anybody do Meth - satan's blood. Aunt Wisdom & Uncle Humor have no respect for your mother after she hauled off & hit you when you were 16 at Our Lady of Mercy on thorazine. What if your child o'd on codein, morphine, pills, heroin? What would you do? Kill yourself? Like pretty Venzuala. Would you have commited suicide if your mother had lived? You had better fear God! You are getting your ass chewed! I got employee of the month at Camel Carriers Trucking Company & volunteer of the year at Amazing Marines Soldiers of the cross - most knowledgable in trivia, 2 who's Who at Zion Egypt Community College. Glory Days & Resumé. You had better get paid for writing this bullshit down. They are going to spit on you at Shop-a-Lot #666 #999. What if Godspell dies she is 80 & doesn't believe there's a hell.

The Bible is confusing you. What do these parables mean? Cleanliest is next to godliness. True Blue Fu. Who is the anti-Christ? Get a job! Take this Shop-a-Lot job & shove it! You have flunked every test. Pray before you faint! There are perverts! You feel sorry for yourself, Mae. Why don't you try to be thankful. I feel the Earth move under my feet. I feel the sky tumbling down. Sing a song! Mae Psalm was my favorite daughter at Shop-a-Lot - beautiful long blonde hair, big green eyes married to Little Jesus. They both got fired, got unemployment & new jobs. Theo, my beloved cat is choking. Holy God, Holy God, hear my prayer.

Your mother ____er, you had better not kill my cat. You have killed everything else. I am sorry I thought that! You had better not mess with me. I love you! Where is the mercy? I know God. Prayer is the wireless connection. You have a smart mouth, Mae. I AM doing everything in my power to keep this world alive.

Satan is the one killing everything. Fasting & prayer gets out demons. In God we trust. Do you swear on that Bible to tell the whole truth, nothing but the truth so help me God. Look what they are doing to the children - sticking dicks penises in their mouths on jury duty. I cannot believe a word they're saying. Rape, drugs, sodomy, stealing, flagrant fathers. $12.50 a day. I can hear dead people. You can achieve the impossible with God. You & your Aunt Baba are talking. Do everything she says to do. Smile! How can you kill a child? That is wicked. You had better get that WIC exactly right at Shop-a-Lot #666 #999. You cannot stand the name Alice. Her husband is buying bullets with her discount card. You had to turn everything in. That was one of the hardest things you have ever done getting that $1500 from America when you were fired for solicitating a book. You had to take care of Compassion - Ruthie.

God blessed you for that. She was a hippy, saved, had been to Woodstock, collected gargoyls, dragons, had 2 dauchsands, parrot, smoked, & drank beer, did not go to church. Compassion went straight to Heaven. Who told these lies on you? You are a prayer warrior. It is very, very cold waiting for the snow. A bird's warble is more important than a stateman's speech. You are so angry at Micah, gay brother for telling on me when you were 50. God cannot stand nurse practicioner Hope & your so called friend Joy. Scorpios are mean! They are ruled by the sex loins & read Cosmopolitan together. That is a nasty magazine. Adam & Eve is the most disgusting, nastiest store I have ever been in.

You are shaking like shit on that pedestal in front of God. You are throwing a manic-depressive bi-polar, paranoid schizophrenic fit. A boy, girl called IT. When you were 2, Micah had double pneumonia & mom was smoking around an oxygen tent 106° temperature. You stabbed him in the face with a pencil, hit him in the head accidently with a teeter totter. How many times have you almost lost your gay beloved saintly brother? You cannot stand the good-looking neighbor boy next door, Free Will. & he can't stand you because you won't be with him. Your mother almost made you kill yourself. You are petrified of Friday the 13th. 13 is a bad luck number. Thunder is the sound of hoof beats in Heaven. It's hard to feel blessed when you don't feel your best! Thank you God for understanding & clearing that matter up. You have to be a bit too kind in this world to be kind enough. Please relax & take care. You're remembered in prayer. Per Joy's husband, Methodist - chicken is a lot like pussy, if it smells bad you don't eat it. You had better help French lady from the Amazing Marines Soldiers of the Cross.

The only people who can help me is Joseph Abraham, millionaire plumber, Micah, my gay brother & Aaron, my deceased best friend Scorpio True/Trust/Truth's Sagitarius husband. Who was that little 3 year old girl - "I want a doggy. I want a daddy. He'll rape me." The delusion has disappeared. Deers have got to be the most magnificent creature I have ever seen. There is no way I could shoot a deer, fawn. These animals are sacred to me. Praise God from where all blessings flow. Praise Him all creatures here below. Praise Him above yea heavenly host. Praise Father, Son, & Holy Ghost. You need some holy blessed water & wine to repent. Your eyes have blessed the wine - 99 by ToTo one of my favorite bands.

It is 2-14-21. Happy Valentine's Day! It is Emmanuel & Cheer's (soul sister's) birthdays - both fellow Aquariuses. I believe in Cupid - mischievious little cherib. This crazy book gay religious son of a preacher keeps sending me tons of kind cards because I am on home kidney dialysis which I hate, but have no other choice. This nice man is praying for me. It is way too cold today. He is manic-depressive, bi-polar too. I am praying for him, too. Is he on meth like brother Micah thinks. God works in mysterious ways & has a funny way of showing His LOVE. LOVE & LAUGH.

I love my cat, Theo, a bushel & a peck, a hug around the neck. I will be a poor shepherd in Heaven. It is a day to celebrate LOVE. - One of my favorite holidays - today & July 4th. - the birth & freedom of the U.S.A. Mama Mia was a sad & happy movie with Meryl Streep. Jericho had to fix my air-conditioner. Pray for these books to sell. Be careful you may end up in my novel. All the names have been changed to protect the innocent & the guilty.

Gift/gifted was my good Pisces talented friend who died at 49. She was the prettiest girl I have ever seen & we argued over who was Aragorn & who was Gandolf by J.R.R. Tolkien. Did she die of cancer? I want to talk to her & say good-bye. Why did God make hornets? You want your god ____ money. Universe charged you $1400 to type crazy check. A masterpiece. Why is this home kidney dialysis so complicated?

Abortion is wrong. The judges black illegitimas child. That black man killed the captain cheerleader's mother & sister. The smart black cheerleader has to run for her life under secret identity. Lock your doors! Lover Helper, my 2nd cousin got raped by the judge's son. - Faith's oldest, pretty Aries daughter teacher. It is 0700 on 9-11-2020 - a day to remember. Early to bed, early to rise makes a man healthy, wealthy & wise per Ben Franklin. Light a magic candle for those soldiers. Micah's birthday is 9-15. We are going out to eat in this corona virus SH#T if I am still alive. Why do you sneeze so much in the mornings? _____ ! Who are you for President of the United States? Trump or Biden? The kidney nurses, social worker, dietician, Dr. Blessings have treated you like a queen goddess of the office. Eat protein. You want to be rich & famous. You got called an air head at Camel Carrier Trucking Company & you bought him a douche bag for the fat preacher. Isaac whom I loved did not fire you. Isaac used to play funny, dirty tricks on me - the Italian Stallion. Isaac died in his sleep, had twins one severely retarded boy & did not drink. Isaac made me laugh. We used to give gag gifts at Christmas. I was on the grand jury. I cannot believe my ears. Judas Iscariot who had a satanic bible in blood used to tell me jokes trying to cheer me up. Jezebell, the best trucking coordinator & Mexico used to pick up men. That's when I dated Bartholomew, a truck driver. He was the best sex & went thru 3 blondes. Damascus, my friend, has a feeding tube. Oh how hard I pray. God has killed France who died from cirrhosis of the liver, Isaac, Honesty, Heart, Alexis, Gift/gifted, a man with an inoperable brain tumor. I loved those people! Who is next? Alexis was my best friend who went blind from diabetes. I cannot stand that disease. Hong Kong had a horrible car wreck & the nurses clapped when she held one finger up. Humility was my favorite friend. We used to go to a country bar, drink rum & coke, go to Gatlinburg, she was a great story teller & yes God can see us. So many people have died that I loved. Oh Lord, open my eyes to see what is beautiful. My mind to know what is true. My heart to love what is good. For God's sake. Amen. Faith & Aunt Abundance were rich snobs - jaywalkers. Mae is tired of being snobbed. The cherib angels with trumpets have already taken my spirit to Heaven & all I have left is a body. Peace came over me. It is time to go. Dead people are coming back to you in your dreams. They are alive & resurrected.

These angels are flipping me out! Cherish the good! Charity had the balls to ask for your stimulus check because you are not for Trump. This world is evil. Nothing is for free. Ecclesiastes drunk lesbian alcoholic wants to beat the crap out of Joy. You would like to kill her. Scorpios are mean! What if your son was atheist? You had better beware of the devil. Mae is a martyr.

Season Marie Raphael. What are you doing community service for at the Amazing Marines Soldiers of the Cross? You had better feed poor people. Hide the knife. This _____ing phone doesn't work & favorite cousin Job's phone lines are tapped because he

35

is selling cocaine & oxycotten. Money comes & goes but donot let it determine your happiness. You cannot be too rich, too skinny, or too young. Job was a lawyer. His oldest son, Sodom, got arrested for selling cocaine, & Job said he knew nothing about it. Sodom, a lawyer, had to go to jail for child support, married a devil woman, had 3 sons & now is clean & remarried. He got his shock probation. Look how many murders have been in Zion, Egypt because of money & drugs. You had better not lie under oath so help me God. Rev. Daniels says touch the loving white light orb that both you & Joy saw. Whose deceased soul was it?

Jesus is protecting you. You gave St. Peter a candle. He let you right into Heaven. The streets are paved in gold. Jesus is the light of the world. God is a great god & he is a jealous god. LOVE is not jealous. You had better do everything He says. You are scared to death of the commode. Tara adobe abode is a haunted house. Those people are having sex with angels. What if you were turned into a pillar of salt? Lutheran was the classiest black lady at Camel Carriers Trucking Company. You want to hold her hand. The tree cutter that ripped me off wants to know if I believe in sex - sexual harassment. He demolished my dog pen that cost $1600, left the wood, & took my money. God's ice storm killed all my trees. I was so mad! Armaggedon was a junkie killed by a drunk driver - MADD - mothers against drunk drivers. He was a bad, bad man. What are the 60 things God says about sex? You have to be married. My gay faggot brother Micah has been very ugly in sharing. You had better be careful what you wish for. Will there be World War III? You are too scared to cry, Mae. God is a jealous god. You got employee of the month when you worked at Camel Carriers Trucking Company. 1994 was when your mom passed away from throat cancer & they gave you $300. $5,000 severence pay. Barnabus & Luke got fired. I loved the prophet John the Baptist! You spat on your mom's, Uncle Protection, & Faith's graves & then you cried. You want your brother dead for putting you in Jabosite Haven when you were 50 & calling your book Jeans/genes stupid. You are a cold hearted bitch, Mae. Everything will be okay. You're with Jay Disobedience that died when he was 40. There is SH#T all over you, Mae. Micah is not saved, reborn again. Touch the white loving, healing light - orbs of deceased souls. Abra Abra ca damra. I want to reach out & grab ya. Uncle Protection broke Aunt Beautiful Patience's rib hugging her too hard. I thought he was going to break my hands. They are kissing under the mistletoe. Uncle Protection almost raped me - "I am not Baba!" If you need anything, call Joy. She thinks Blessed is mentally ill for giving up her 3 children to her mother in North Carolina for a year. 8-4-2 year old darling children. Blessed has a new boyfriend & looks horrible. - No teeth, overweight & dirty clothes. She was almost sent to House of Horrors/Wax because her ex-husband said she had guns & needles. Pray, Mae. Was she on Prosac? I would be afraid I would kill somebody on that SH#T. It's not the end of the world yet! That Mayan calender had never been wrong in 12-21-12. Joy's atheist son in the Air Force, Baptist's son's baby girl is due 6-14 - a Gemini. Charity & you do not agree on politics, love, & life, ghosts. Is astrology satanic?

The peace of strength, the strength of peace. Look how cyan blue deceased LOVE's face is. You had to get your stomach pumped because you almost O'd on valium when you were 16. How many times has God saved your life?! You are dutch. Get these spiders off me! You are in love with Canaan. You had better get the vaccine for COVID-19.

LOVE casteth out all fear. Your mom is drinking beer. You are an alcoholic. Look what happened at Mammoth Cave. You & deceased LEO girlfriend & you are in deep SH#T. - Persistance R.N. nurse. Watch that purse! That Catholic psychic fortune teller is the prettiest girl you ever saw. Is there an evil spirit following you around? She would not tell you who it was. Do you believe in Tarot cards? Queen of Pentacles. Maebelle was a rich bitch, social butterfly. She is in pergatory. Whatever you do, do not touch her gay daughter's Poinsettia's brass bed with your hands. Companion, her son of a bitch son was mean. Reverant/respect thinks my art is 192. A masterpiece.

At Camel Carriers Trucking Company, Iran & Iraq used to fight. Iran called Iraq little rich boy & Iraq called a nun a bitch in Catholic school. I think he got a whipping for that. I used to throw gun to him to keep him from shaking my cubicle.

Iran is retired now fat & sassy. Judge & be not judged. Hungary, co-ordinator, was the best-looking man I have ever seen. I had no desire to be with him because he was so naughty. This was a hard job for 17 glorious years. I was the gopher. India got a D.U.I. at the Christmas party. She was wearing a beautiful white & gold dress. In jail she was the fairy princess. She was big & wore beautiful dresses. She will not see me because all I have to say about these people is good things. Mom used to say, does the truth hurt?

Lutheran was black. Halo & Heaven was black & I loved them. We were the blues sisters. You've got to do what you've got to do. I hated that female vice-president who wanted to fire me because I had been incarcerated 4 times. Camel Carriers Trucking Company moved to the sunshine state. It was all the commander & chief's, Lucifer's fault. You loved the executive president of the company, John the Baptist. Snowden Zodiac Spy was my German shepherd husky that the bastard neighbor made me get rid of take to the Humane Society. I miss my dog! Calvin Klein. The dog went to obedience school for $500, crashed thru the sliding glass window, had 15 stitches in her leg. Blood was everywhere! That window cost me $450. Calvin Klein had a cone on her head, tore up everything,

& I hope & pray she got adopted. I thought she was going to kill my cat, Theo. I am on home kidney dialysis. Peace was agnostic & died at 89. Life after death.

I had a dream that I was working at this strange place. There was a girl woman from Camel Carriers Trucking Company, & a girl from Shop-a-Lot #666 #999. There were about 10 girls & we were putting dirt, soil in tiny cardboard wares. I received a dozen beautiful red roses & the card said Love, Gideon. One girl said he had been divorced for a year. I had mixed, confused feelings about starting this flame up again. How did he know. Where I worked? Free will, good-looking next door neighbor, got beat till he was bruised with a paddle by the black vice-principal at Zion, Egypt High School, streaked & is a jerk. I have no desire to be with him. I love his 80 year old Capricorn mother Godspell. They have been good to you. I love being treated like a queen Goddess of the Office. This world is going crazy right now in 2021 because of Corona 19 virus.

I am tired of being called dumb & stupid.

RESUMÉ

Camel Carriers Trucking Company 17 years. Switchboard operator, money desk clerk, liason to Com Data. Moved to the sunshine state.

Clothing factory - picker - quit.

Shop-a-Lot - 10 years, 4 star cashier, people greeter - fired for solicitating a book.

Zion, Egypt Community College
3.6 g.p.a. 1981

Associate in Arts (all the prerequisites to R.N. Nursing), Associate in Applied Science (secretarial administration), English 101, 102, Speech, Psychology, Biology, Sociology, Typing, Shorthand, Accounting I & II, Office Management, Medical Terminology

Zion, Egypt High School 1976
Bicentenniel year graduate. 3.4 gpa. 5 year cheerleader, Beta Club, Pep Club, M Club, Secretary-Treasurer of Art class.

Tawny Mae Harris

References:

Judge Wonderful Tahiti
270-821-1896

Peace - Art Teacher
270-821-6662

Messiah - Gay organist at Hebrew Tabernacle Episcopal Church
270-821-3674

Volunteer of the Year at the Amazing Marines Soldiers of the Cross

Paul, the con-artist, drug pusher is dead from aides or a stroke. French lady got my telephone number from the Capricorn lady at the laundry mat. She is beautiful for 88 years old & distressing. Her kids will not help her. I do not know where she lives. I cannot help myself much less someone else. I met her at the Soldiers of the Cross Amazing Marines. Maybe, I can find out where she lives. I love her & it is hard to understand her french accent. I donot drive out of town. I only make $1200 on social security disability. I will pray for someone to help her. Angel I, Compassion, Isabella, Jehosphat, Cheer, Sunshine all passed away at Shop-a-Lot #666 #999.

Aunt Abundance poured milk on her daughter's Faith's head. Leah was whipped into religion & is in Crusade for Christ. She is big & said Micah & I were not considered a part of the family. Her daughter, Garden of Gethsamene is beautiful. Rebekka is an Aquarius & has 2 darling grandchildren. Is it the end of the world - Corona virus? Freddie Mercury in queen died from aides. Paul owes me money. The lithium has shut down my kidneys & home kidney dialysis is scarey. Theology & Tangerine are my precious cat children. I should have named her Mittens or Scamper; but she has a religious name. Theo is a tabby cat with green eyes & Tangerine is an outside orange & white cat with yellow eyes. Tangerine has disappeared. Theo sleeps with me & is very, very sweet.

You had better stand up for your self, Mae. You had no idea what you were doing when you got an abortion. That is murder, and I regret it so much & paid dearly. Micah is a stupid queer faggot & does not pray. At Camel Carriers Trucking Company, Herod the bastard president had a pink slip black Friday lay-off. I did not get laid off. The vice-presidents are gospells - Matthew, Mark, Luke, & John. I liked Mark. His wife died. She was so pretty & her son was the editor of the paper. When he was a boy, he liked to play with snakes. My picture was in the newspaper twice for the Amazing Marines Soldiers of the Cross as Grinch at Christmas volunteer of the year. Lutheran was the classiest black lady I have ever met, & I have total respect for her skin color. She was over the switchboard. Halo & Heaven were my best black friends. Halo used to give me wake-up calls which I appreciated very much. Heaven & I were the blues sisters. I would have that cigarette hanging out of my mouth driving my canary yellow Impala car. They all gave me an apartment shower. I worked 5½ days a week. Toward the end, I worked Sundays. They did not want to pay overtime. When Mom died on 2-18, 1994, Dad wanted you to sell the house & get an efficiency apartment. Aunt Wisdom disagreed. Tara is my spooky, haunted adobe abode. Beloved Aunt Wisdom's last words to me where don't sell your house & don't have children.

Messiah, the gay organist that passed away said I was going to rot in the house & gave me $60 when I got fired from Shop-a-Lot #666 #999.

I loved Martin Luther King. He had a dream - if we don't start loving, we will start dying.

Migger day. Soul, the black elderly lady that cleaned our house was my favorite. Soul liked Mom the best because she was so awnry. I liked Scorpio, Aunt Beautiful Patience the best, then Aunt Wisdom, then Mom Loyal Dedication, then Aunt Abundance. I miss my aunts! I am off on Tuesdays & Saturdays from my home kidney dialysis. I feel so sorry for myself. Mom used to call me poor pitiful pearl. I want sympathy. Jabosite Haven was a horrible mental hospital & I expect to get every last dime back. Mom wore a button - who the ____ knows & who the ____ cares. I keep getting harassing calls that say my social security number is fraugulent & they are cancelling my social security. Is this fraud? It is a scam & they are going straight to hell. Mind your own business MYOB. God binds broken hearts. You are Catholic as hell. Mammy was a wise old bird.

Think positive & positive things will come to you. Think negative & negative things will come. Hope for the best & expect the worst. Hersheys Kiss Licorice - JuJu is the outside big black cat that is limping. Felix is the other big black & white cat that I feed every day. I love cats! 2-18-21 There is 10 inches of snow on the ground. I can't wait till it melts! Pray for your self # 5. There were 2 little old ladies sitting on a bench waiting for the bus & it was running late. One old lady said I've been sitting here so long my butt is asleep. The other old lady said yes, I heard it snoring. LOVE & LAUGH! Laughter is good medicine. Do not have sex in your mother's bed. I can't have sex anyway. I have a catheder in my stomach. I love rum - pina coladas. Why are you scared paranoid of everything? Is it your mental illness? Opals are bad luck to wear if they are not your birth stone. I think opals are so pretty. Garnet is my birthstone.

I am not scared of living I am just scared of living. I am not so scared of dying I am just scared of dying. Touch the white loving light - orb - a deceased soul. Dr. Jain was my first kidney doctor. He said it was adwil. I wanted to die on my lithium; but, he wanted me to live. Dr. Glory, a beautiful Afghanistan female doctor told me I had 23% left of my kidneys, you live long life - enjoy! You write book after this book. You be infatuated with many men - enjoy! Then there was the kidney doctor that wanted to know if I could pee. Dr. Shepherd, whom I was in love with, got a terrible divorce & moved away to take care of his mother. Now, I see Dr. Blessings that does not know what this world is coming to? Corona pandemic. I have changed my mind. I want to live. All my friends are dying. They come back to me in my dreams. There is a dead black bird outside in the snow.

Everything will be okay. God is not responsible for these deaths. It is satan killing people. God only takes the best - Messiah, gay organist at Hebrew Tabernacle Episcopal Church. Sarah Israel is gone too - a good, good lady - Mose's wife. Why did God make germs?

Remember the good times! Micah, my gay brother, is a good time. I am very confused about the Bible. I read GOD CALLING 25 times. Satan is so vain. I am NOT vain. He is trying to crush my head. Cry! Diary of a dead man, mad man. You had better get a sword! You had better not mess with Mother Nature! Jayden "Care" Arthur, co-manager who got fired wrote Honor my fully loaded sacrifice at Shop-a-Lot #666 #999. Where lies the soul of Adam Lot? Jayden was too young for you, Mae. Charity, Gemini, acts like her SH#T don't stinks! Feed that ghost! Kindness & Gracie Bathsheba from Shop-a-Lot #666 #999 are 2-faced CSM's - customer sales managers.

God, Yahweh, Jehovah I AM THAT I AM is on your side. You thanked Him for another day. My aura & my halo are temporially out of order.

Cauldron, Cauldron
forgive, forgotten
will you be pardoned?

You are supposed to forgive you enemies 777 times. That is virually impossible. Thomas was an airplane pilot for Camel Carriers Trucking Company & I absolutely loved that man. The building has been torn down. All that remains is the computer room. Where have all my friends gone? Ho Ho Ho - got to go - got to deliver presents to the kids you know. Santa saw a pretty lady. HEY HEY HEY - got to stay. Can't get up the chimney with my dick this way. You are having a spell. Your mother put you in jail. Did she go to hell? Your mother said she was sorry calling you a fat hog & thunder thighs & you did not accept her apology. Babylon has fallen. Read every religious book you can get your hands on! Mae has been called wicked. Moses does not think you are wicked that you are a great lady. I love Moses! You are being slapped across your face till your nose bled. Mae fought every battle for her child. Isaiah got kicked out of the army for being manic-depressive. They treat you like dogs!

Private Benjamin - you had better not commit suicide. It happens mostly in the spring. Why?

I am going to hunt you down & kill you Mae. You are not in your right mind. What is this world coming to?! You made a C in English & Speech - 3A's 15 hours. Micah has got the littliest dick I have ever seen.

I went to the laundry mat today 9-12-20 & these mean little boys said quit staring at me. I was sitting outside in the rain smoking a cigarette & a barefooted sweet 10 year old girl walked up & said you look like you have no money & offered me $5.00. I refused but my faith has been restored. I want that child! Girls are sweet. Boys are mean. What if you

43

had a penis, what would you do? That is where men's brains are located. Torana Bobbit is my hero. Look at that dick on that bug that splashed the car window. Everybody is so pretty & you are so ugly. Canaan says you are a dumb, stupid, & mean. Mae has been an absolute angel since God talked to her. Thunder is the sound of hoof beats in Heaven. There is going to be a big fight over who gets President - Biden or Trump? I hope I am around to see Trump get beat. Vote Democrat! Why is pee yellow? I don't like the colors yellow, orange, or red. I like lavender, pink, blue, purple, then black, then brown why did God make mosquitos & ticks? You have so many questions. Are God's eyes as blue as the skies? Do everything Moses tells you to do. You almost killed yourself working at Shop-a-Lot #666. Gracie Bathsheba & Kindness CSM's customer service managers are control freaks. The belt is child abuse. Do not provoke your children to anger, wrath. Joy's atheist son, Baptist is married & doing well in the Air Force. Her prodigal son is awesome & you had better not say _____ you. Mom had a fire in the oven cooking meat loaf & bacon. _____ you! _____ you! I'm calling the fire department! You are so Catholic, Mae. You had better repent of your sins. The wages of sin is death. Calm-not speed. I hated Shop-a-Lot #666 because of the liars & backstabbers. Joy cometh in the morning. Pray before you faint. Micah is strange - he likes graveyards. You are filled with the Holy Ghost. He has a personality. Simon was a sorceror. He is my favorite. St. Jude, Andrew, Job, Paul are all my favorites. You are talking in tongues when you were sleepwalking. Whatever you do, do not wake them up, they will go into shock. I stuck my tongue out at Mom for waking me up & laughing. Maebelle hugged me. She was a wealthy Sagittarius. Rich people don't make it to Heaven. Blessed are the poor. TGIF - Thank goodness I am from Kentucky. There are a bunch of catatonic crazy people. Cousin Faith's daughter, Omnipotence, went to rehab for drinking & Zanex, good cook & got married. We were not invited to the wedding. Quote Psalm 23. Make new friends but keep the old. One is silver & the others gold. There was an ambulance & a box fell off of it. The car behind it & picked it up. It had 3 toes in it so who did they call - the tow truck. Your mother wants you to be strong. Shooting herself was wrong. Micah stole every penny out of that jar, messed - up my room, broke the candles of my favorite angels because I told on him for quitting MacDonalds. He pulled the fire alarm & white dust came down & they had to close MacDonalds for 3 hours. Mae will get her revenge. Paybacks are hell! Listen to the birds. Birds of a feather fly together. Tested curse is talking about you like a dog. Pray for yourself: #5. They are killing Eagles. How much did those trees cost to be cut down? They are sacred talking to each other in Latin. Hope, the nurse practitioner Scorpio that told all kinds of lies on me that I hated is no longer working at Penny royal - Dr. Sam. I was handing out Prayer Warrior books at Trover Clinic, slept on the couch cause I was afraid I'd be raped, went to the door naked. All lies! I hope she dies from Corona virus. Micah & Joy will pay for Jebusite Haven. I cannot stand Dr. Trojan. Beware of the devil!

You & Gift/gifted are smoking pot & sneaking out of the house at 2 am walking clear across town in the dark. She was your best friend! A good Pisces that passed away guitarist at 49 - computer programmer for 30 years at Camel Carriers Trucking Company - green peace, rescued cats, pretty hippy, your wrists are killing you.

That is the worst news you have ever had in your life. Do you want to go home? Why is Gracie Bathsheba in the wheel chair trying to be nice to me at Shop-a-Lot #666 #999? She is a wolf in sheep's clothing & Satan I Ezekiel hopes she dies. How many times has Gracie Bathsheba sued Shop-a-Lot? Those kidney people are treating you like queen Goddess of the Office. Micah is a saint. He says God says love me or go to hell if you are atheist. He says God is more understanding & loving than that. The bone doctor at the church says hackers are jack asses. Mental telepathy, 6th sense, clairvoyance is a gift. - the shining. You hurt God's feelings. You donot understand about the LOVE. It all ends in a confusing laugh. Why is God doing this to me?

In 1974 when I was 16, I did not go out for cheerleading because I wanted to do drugs. Wrong answer.

LOVE O'd on morphine & died & I threw a hissy fit, od'd on valium. I wanted to read my poems at LOVE's funeral & ran away from home. Uncle Humor pulled me out of the Volkswagon. They were very cruel to me. 60 minutes came down & interviewed a boy who used to party: but, is now a preacher. I met his younger brother at the Amazing Marines Soldiers of the Cross doing community service for a D.U.I. in Florida. He was very talented, sang & played guitar & lied about drinking beer. He said, "Mae, you had better be careful drinking on those psyche meds. Gift/gifted got busted for drugs & they put me on the 6th floor sent me to Our Lady of Mercy in Nazareth, Egypt on thorazine with a bunch of crazy people, a Catholic Mental Hospital runned by nuns. If you're not crazy when you go in, you're crazy when you get out.

Sisters nuns Mary Alexis & Alexis Mary were my English & History tudors. I have total respect for a nun. I thanked God for my eyes when I was on acid L.S.D. Flash backs are hell! What's that spell? Candle light all a glow. Tell me what you know. The devil is out to get you. My girl statue holding a cat - Starsky Michelle Mystique, my naked lady statue - Queen Elizabeth, my angel statues - Francesca, Gabriel, Gardenia & Chassie. Isaac at Camel Carriers Trucking Company used to put a dildo at the bottom of his pants making us laugh - WOP Itallian Stallion. There was a skeleton with interchangeable sexual body parts & he tapped my titty with a pencil. I cried when he died in his sleep. Isaac was vice-president in the executive department & I was money desk, clerk, comdata liason. Drink beer for Isaac.

Can dead people see us? Do they fly around like spirits or are they asleep. They are alive & resurrected. Isaac's sexual harassment was funny & I did everything Isaac told me to do. I was the gopher. The 4 vice-presidents are the 4 gospels. Matthew, Mark, Luke, & John. I liked Mark the best. The Amazing Marines Soldiers of the Cross breaks my heart. Homeless people, community service, poor starving people, people that cannot afford their light bill. I was volunteer of the year. Keep them in your prayers. People call me crazy. Hungary is the best-looking man that used to pick me up in the snow. Buddha picked me up, too. Winter is my least favorite season. Zion, Egypt is a wicked town. Grieve yourself to death. Be grateful! You had better not tread on me.

Blessed are the poor. Shop-a-Lot #666 is calling you idiots. Scott Alex is going to sue them. He told God to kiss his ass! Look how many people they have fired. Ms. Mary USA, prophet, Jayden, Blessed, kind Amos, James I, Ms. Longevity, Cheer, King of the Jews, Mae. That was a blessing in disguise because of your kidneys. You are robbing the cradle. God is on your side. Whatever you do, do not _____ up! Paul, my ex-boyfriend died of aides. Look what happened to Janis Joplin, Jimmy Hendrix, John Lennon, Robin Williams, Freddy Mercury, Bill Cosby. St. Jude is my favorite. Do you hear voices? What does this dream mean? That girl is biting your hand. You do not understand this parable. Something terrible is going to happen. You are kin to the sleeping prophet. Edgar Cayce by marriage. Do everything that Holy Spirit tells you to do. Everything came true. Look at the bloody red moon. What if your child o'd on codeine? You had better not do meth - satan's blood. God is going to bless the hell out of you, Mae. There are perverts in this dangerous town of Zion, Egypt. Mae is very superstitious. Tomorrow is gay brother Micah's birthday 9-15-20. He is 61 - a senior citizen & a saint. He had better not call me spacey. You know nothing about computers. You are a cougar. The world took sides. Get a sword! Mack the knife. People are going crazy during this corona virus. This has been the worst year I can remember.

What has that fortune teller seen in that crystal ball? Look what drunk gay Red Sea did. He wanted to marry mother, laid on top of her in front of me & called me a brat. Red Sea wondered why witness's sister & I were not models. I am only 5'4". You have to be 5'7". You went straight to Heaven. Mae cannot stand Mellaril & Tegretol. The lithium shut down her kidneys. You ought to sue that doctor Sweden psychiatrist if he wasn't dead. How many people have died in Our Lady of Mercy? The boy hung himself with a coat hanger & really wanted to die. You pray all day! What would you do if you found a hyper needle? Shoot yourself like Mom did? No, take her to re-hab. Your guardian angel's name is Caleb which means dog.

Look how rich Billy Graham got. He was the greatest evangelist of all time! You are a power angel. From sea to shining sea. You have total respect for Catholic & Episcopalian nuns. Linda Ronstandt has Parkinson's disease Red rover, red rover, we want you to come over. Welcome to the real dog eat dog world, Ms. Harris, electronic warfare. Cheer was the smartest black soul sister that passed away at 57. All she wanted was my food stamp card. Cheer got fired from Shop-a-Lot #666 #999 for stealing. Everybody loved funny Cheer. What kind of disease did she have? I pray I don't get sued. Light that candle 7 times for good luck. Martha was a saggy titty blonde bitch that was firing everybody. Shop-a-Lot was such a dirty company to work for. I did not get my unemployment. Amoré is the one that fired me. They will pay. All those people were liars & backstabbers. Why do people use me? If I were Ecclesiastes, I would have taken Happiness to court for spending all her $7,000 back pay social security. I would have never spent that money. God said thank you for your candle-lighting faith. I AM coming down to save you from poverty & hate. There is your mother's ghost in your house, Tara abode. Get out! Get off my cloud nine. I had a dream I was painting condo balconies white. Peace was naked with a towel. You could see her butt & boobs. It was repulsive. Peace got a check from the community college for $171.00 for reading to a tutor. Terry Brown got her that job. I said I can't do manual hard work with a catheder in my stomach but I can do mental work. Mom is supposed to take me to a clothing surplus store. We go in a pet store & Peace buys a dog tag for a dollar something. At the pet store, the cute young blonde that worked there said 3 trip leasors were awesome called her baby. Trip leasors drivers like blondes. Then we go to the vet to pick-up art teachers Peace's 2 cats. They are holding them in their arms & this young, long brown haired girl is telling the cats to go to hell, kiss her ass. The girl unbuttons her white jacket & covers up her cleavange. A car comes by & wants to know where one dollar store is & I said go down Franklin Street. We are taking the 2 calm cats to the car. Uriah, the sick diaper bed occult man wanted to sue Joy for hostile work environment. It never happened. He had better not put a diaper on me. The dentist office is treating you like Queen Goddess of the Office. You call Charity every day to check-up on her. I always have vivid dreams sleeping on the couch on Tuesdays & Saturdays. I go to Roses & I don't see anything I want to buy. The math book is in your car & you drive to Mother's office. She has a dimpled chin which is the sign of the devil. Kindness had a dimpled chin. I go to the store walking my dog & Lutheran black lady is there. I lose my purse in a basket.

When I was in Jebosite Haven at 50, they liked my hair & smile. I think I am ugly because of my burned, scarred nose. God said He was sorry for scaring you. You cannot stand to look in the mirror. You used to be so pretty when you were young. God's world is beautiful. Canaan is a good sumaritan, smart, good-looking, knowledgeable, funny Virgo born 9-27. You worship the sunshine. What was the gospel about today? 2-21-21.

Your mother is baking homemade yeast bread on Sunday drinking beer. On God our help in ages past, our hope for years to come who saved us from the stormy blast & helped us carry on. Hope flourishes. Doubt flees. Feed the Hobo a sandwich. What goes around comes around. Micah is hateful when he's busy. You are waiting to hear the frogs sing in the spring. God said yes to your deal of not drinking & driving.

Judge & be not judged. The last enemy you have to conquer is death. Jesus was a man of sorrors acquainted with grief - a craven motal. God, why have you abanoned me? Build me up butter cup, don't break my heart. In the year 25, 25 - it's a wonder we are still alive. I would swim the deepest seas, climb the highest mountains just to be with you - Grassroots. Micah tore up Aunt Baba's stereo & I almost got blamed for the destruction. I will never leave you or forsake you. The Graphein in creative writing class - my favorite old maid teacher. Here is the winning poem by a beautiful girl friend in Zion, Egypt High School 1976. Today is filled with yesterdays filled with golden fields of mid-summer flowers & gold filled bottles of wine no soon to be forgotten. This is the matching face of the country side begin to dry & wither. Veto tombs scattered from a sweet storm. I cannot see to read the rest. We used to ride to school together, smoke pot together & play in the snow at the park. Those were the Glory Days! Micah is a mean, mean little boy & he lied to his grandmother about your mother being with that junkie nurse Japan. You did everything your grandmother told you to do. You had better beware of crazy mon-mon men. You had better take the bitter with the sweet. Go live with your father. Your mother is provoking a big fight. Bully for you! You can go to jail for bullying. That girl does not like you down at the Amazing Marines soldiers of the Cross because you gave her little Pisces sister a cross necklace. Trash goes down there.

Dolly Parton wanted to be like trash & look how famous she got. I miss the funny majors! I love sea gulls, snow seals, guinea pigs, horses, fawns, dear, dogs, cats & fish, turtles, angels, starfish, vases, dolls. What if you thought you were possessed by the devil? Dr. Fable, a good dentist shot himself because of that. His beautiful cheerleader daughter had a horrible car wreck & almost died. Mary Marie, class favorite, Humility's daughter had a blister baby that died. Humility was a famous story teller, single dances, Gatlinburg, & she is so mad at Aunt Abundance. You have been called every name in the book. Look what happened to Amelia Airhart in the Bermuda Triangle. Angel I & Isabella were 2 great ladies from Shop-a-Lot #666 #999 that died young. Only the good die young. Micah wants to know what you're living for? You're smoking! Now that is the meanest thing you can say. Aunt Abundance said I was negative & not going to make it. Hope for the best, expect the worse. My best Scorpio girlfriend, True/Trust/Truth who died from a hoskiens tumor at 42 said you will have to show her you will make it. How can you think positive with all the negative things in the world? Micah's 61 birthday dinner cost $63.48. Be a cheerful giver. I was full after the strawberry dacquiri, salad, & fried mushrooms with honey mustard sauce. I could not eat the catfish & onion rings & fed it to the racoons. Micah had an 8 oz. sirloin medium rare, asparagus, loaded potato. He ate all of his food. Micah cannot stand the smell of my Chism cigars. We had to wear a mask because of the corona virus. We wasted exspensive food. I had a dream about my funny girlfriend, Humility. We were going to Gatlinburg, TN. I was taping the catheder in my stomach. You wake-up & thought, your dumb ass, you can't go to Gatlinburg, you're on home kidney dialysis. Every hair on your head is counted. You worshipped the ground your grandmother Mammy Wonderful Strength walked on 8-25-1900, a Virgo. My peas. His peas. Her peas. You had better not take the mark of the beast. How many times have you been abandoned? Remember the good times - glory days.

ALL MY CHILDREN

All my children pets are named after jeans or religious names in the book Queen Goddess of the Office. They are beautiful, loving, blessed creatures of God. Charity says I am scared of everything but I can't help it. Joy, Micah, Hope, Gracie Bathsheba, kindness locked your ass up at Jebosite Haven & you hated them for that at 50. I could not stand Dr. Trojan. I missed my solid white, gold-eyed, beloved cat, Wrangler. Do you think you are normal? Just as normal as anybody else. Wrangler passed away. She loved to have her head & throat rubbed & sleeped, curled-up in my lap. Wrangler was a fighter, my favorite 8 year old cat & I spent $350 on my credit card trying to save her. My halo is temporarily out of order! Oh, how I cried for my bewitching white cat. God gives. God takes away. Death is so mean. Vengeance is mine saith the Lord. Do not piss an Aquarius off! God loves peace-loving hippies. 1-2-3-4 we don't like this stinking war! I am a lover not a fighter. Fight depression like a plague. Pray for understanding not riches & you will be blessed. I am buying you a stairway to Heaven. Meth is death. The dead spirits, ghosts are in your house. Tara adove, abode. You are a prayer warrior. What does raped by the spirit mean? Canaan says my God is a __ ing asshole & he would make a poor preacher tearing the Old Testament in half, throwing it away, Billy Graham is a bastard. I love my God! You had better not break up any marriages. Drink sangria wine & repent. Take time to be holy.

You are in absolute shock. Look what shock treatment does to you. You cannot remember anything. Who is Argentina? Beware of Virgos! You wanted to marry Benjamin Zebidiah, the heating & cooling man 9-1. There is a God! You had better spit everyone of those pills out of your mouth. You are petrified of pit bulls. Forgiveness' mother, Ms. Judgement is rolling over in her grave. I. U. D.'s are dangerous! Your life (live in forever eternity) is in danger. Forgiveness is a Scorpio clean freak. Why me? God has perfect timing. Joy is wining & dining you. Be patient! Enchilados were your favorite that your mom cooked. You miss her cooking & that's all. Drinking is a drug - depressant. L. S. D., acid, mescaline, pot is a halloagenic, cocaine is a stimulant. Look how famous Stevie Nix got. Look how famous Princess Di is. I look like a tree & that dog hiked it's leg & pissed on me. Look at the naked butt picture Luke at Camel Carriers Trucking Company had on his wall. Everybody got laid off or fired & nobody moved to Louisiana. You are a hero, Mae, & they are treating you like a queen Goddess of the office. Where is Atlantis? Don't worry, be happy! Are you sunshine? You love that nun - Dolomine. Is God cruel? No, God is loving-kindness - my favorite virtue. Stand up for your self, Mae. You are innocent until proven guilty. You have been stripped of everything, treated like a criminal, beaten with a belt, slopped till your nose bled, cussed - out. Your mother is a devil - worshipper - you are not satan's daughter. You are not a nice devil! You are a Christian and you deserve to be created with respect. There are fake Christians. We will be persucuted, hated, imprisoned, stoned to death for the sake of Jesus Christ. Woe to the pregnant women at the end of times. Kill or be killed.

Impeach Trump! Crosby, still, Nash & young - our house is a very, very fine house with 2 cats in the yard, life used to be so hard, but now everything is easier with you. You have been ostracized from society. What do they call Tiger Woods? Cheetah. Why did God make germs? Are you prejudice? You are going to get your revenge. If our cat doesn't like you. We probably won't either. Wrangler lied in my arms for 2 days when she got spayed & had to drink strawberry milk antibiotics. She used to scratch my legs & I am so glad I did not get her deglawed. Joy is a nice bitch. There are people starving to death. Compassion is coming back to Earth for you. You are angry that Wrangler passed away. You have got to be saved. You are petrified of bats & rats. When I was in grade school, Poinsettia, Maebelle's gay daughter gave us a black poodle. Mom bred her with a silver poodle & she had 6 puppies. Her tit's were shaved & these puppies had to be hand fed. The black poodle got choked on a choaker chain, had a heart attack, fell down the stairs. Micah started laughing. These puppies sold for $225. They all lived. That's been a long time ago. I loved that dog! Mom gave the biggest puppy to Japan, her junkie nurse friend & he got ran over. Echo's desiree. Mother, Loyal Dedication got all kinds of bowling trophies. She was a better lady than you were.

Nobody loves me. Everybody hates me. Go outside & eat worms. Make an effigy & burn it up! Pets are just like children. Then we had an apricot brandy poodle that mother gave away to a farmer who had cancer.

Levi was an Old English sheepdog that I took everywhere. She had heartworms & we gave her arsenic treatments. We had her for 7 years & she was sh#ting blood & we had to put her to sleep. Kitty Kat had a black kitten named Ebony & 3 more kittens - Peppermint, Piper Sweet, & Dolly. The gray cat was my favorite & Dolly got into a car & got killed by the fan belt. Mom look them to a farm & Kitty Kat Tabitha Pepper got run over by a car. Oh, how we cried. The best present I ever got was & black & tan cocker spaniel - Jordache Conner - Jordie & U.C. - ugly cat. I used to bathe Jordie every week in the tub in my bathing suit. Jordie went blind & deaf & I had to put him to sleep. The most pitifullest thing I ever saw was when U.C., the cat had been in remission for cancer for 5 years. She died in the kitchen & mother was crying I took U.C. to the vet & asked her what did it feel like to die. She said soft & fluffy. We had that great hunter cat for 9 years. U.C. used to kill shrews, rabbits, & play with garter snakes. That crazy kook that keeps sending me cards praying for me. Micah thinks he's on meth. Thay gay guy said, "___, Micah! Eat SH#T, bitch!" Micah called the landlord & got him evicted. They are both being mean. Now, let's go on with something more pleasant. When I was 18, I had a calico goldfish named Gorgeous George. I dropped her down the disposal & she got tail rot. I loved that fish! When I worked at Camel Carriers Trucking Company, I got a collie-husky, Lee, for free. I wanted a friendly dog. She was epileptic & I fed her phenobaritrol twice a day for 12 years. Lee was put to sleep in my arms. That was in 2006. She tore up everything in the den & I would read her children's stories before she went to bed. That's when I got Wrangler, my solid white cat with gold eyes. I got a German Shepherd husky, Calvin Klein, 2 years ago that crashed thru the den's sliding glass door & had 15 stitches in her leg. Blood & glass was everywhere! She went to obedience school owned by a policeman for $500.00. The jerk bastard neighbor made me take her to the Humane Society for getting in his yard. I have 2 cats, Theology & Tangerine. Theology poops & pees underneath the bed. Tangerine is an outside cat orange & white. She disappeared. I am a good shepherd. When I was 23, I had a tiny turtle that I loved named Winky. Save the turtles! You have been way too kind to Jesus & God, Mae.

Francesca is your favorite angels. Cousin Faith killed your child & told you to go to the food bank. Death comes in threes. Forgiveness is divine. Get out of my house! Calvin Klein, the German Shepherd husky ate the lawn couch & I slit my hand on the door taking it to the street & had 9 stitches. She killed rabbits, birds, shrews. What would you do? Why did God make spiders & snakes? You are paranoid. Look what Black Sabbath said Is God dead? God is very much alive.

You made a deal with God - no drinking & driving & he will give you money for your books - Jeans/genes, AGORA, crazy check. Don't worry! Be happy! You are married to Jesus! How many brides of the Lord are there? You are filled with the Holy Spirit. Cast it out in everybodies thoughts, hearts, minds, & bodies, souls thru out the land, the universe. Why did God make roaches? Why do we have to die? To be with God & Jesus eternally. When my loving grandmother Mammy Wonderful Strength was alive, we had guppies & snails in a tropicana orange juice jar. Oh, how I loved it when the fish had tiny babies. My grandmother liked Doris Day. I liked Bewitched, Giligan's Island, & Hollywood Squares. Funny Paul Lynn was my favorite. I had a dream that 3 comchecks with no amounts have disappeared off of my desk. It's a good thing you are not working. I thank God every day for disability for manic-depression, paranoid schizophrenia & kidney dialysis. I go to accts. payable & ask them if they received the comchecks. A lady is holding up a pink negligeé. There is a toy black poodle when I am walking up the stairs. Baba Aunt Beautiful Patience is a clerk. I have to tell my boss, Judas Iscariot. They hand me a piece of paper with Team 20 on it & say this driver is canned, gives them the creeps. I ask who is his co-ordinator. She says Team 21. This lady wants me to pay $200 for her tires.

I stole 2 mice from Woolworth's, a brown one & a white one, stuffed them down my bra, put them in a cage, & set them outside. They disappeared. I stole 2 blue bathing suits from a fancy clothing store down town & a can of beer. I do not steal anymore. Stealing is wrong - one of the 10 commandments. I had a tiny lizard & it got lost in the house & mom made me vacuum all the rugs. The doctor burned a non-cancerous place by my nose on my face & left an ugly scar. It bothers me. I am so self-conscious about it. I had to get my tires filled-up at the Ford dealership yesterday. They were nice about it. I lost $1.75 in quarters in the air pump machine that didn't work & went to Krogers to shop for food & toilet paper. I spent $99.70. I got cat food, laundry detergent, milk, 2 teas, 10 gatorades, 15 chicken & steak frozen dinners. My Zanex is not ready till Tuesday 9-22-20. I wore a mask all because of COVID-19. Charity is self-righteous. God is omnipotent - everywhere. Your mother is pulling your hair. You wanted to suffocate her. Believe in the healing power of laughter, love, & prayer. A gay guy that lives in the apt. next to Micah in the house who just lost his lover sends me beautiful cards in the mail. I love him! He loves Halloween. Feed the cats Theo & Tangerine, Juju & Felix. Free Will, the horny next-door neighbor is a gourmet cook & he has a smart mouth. He drove my black Aveo Chevrolet Panther back from out of town.

I thanked him & his beautiful mother, Godspell. She broke her leg. Freewill just wants to come over _____ me & use me. Does he think he's cute? I have given them turkeys, hams from the Amazing Marines Soldiers of the cross & they fix me a dinner. Godspell is under quarantine from the corona virus. What's this world coming to? Zion, Egypt is a very dangerous drug & money town. There has been several murders, stabbings, & shootings. I do not have a gun! If I had a gun, I would probably shoot myself. Up comes the sun! Down comes the dew. Good morning! Good morning the little birds say! Stay 6 feet away!

CLOUD NINE

This is eulogies about all my dead friends & family. Jesus comes with sandals like a thief in the night. Put on your party hat honey, there's a concert on cloud nine. Why is there so much pain & suffering? It is bad luck to be born a duck. The wicked get no rest until they close their eyes for good. Why does God hate me? God does not hate people. He loves everybody! Mae is the favorite. I dreamed mom & I bought a brand new dream house together with a large fenced - in backyard for a dog for $59,900. Mom was an alcoholic & I was a drug addict. God touched me when I was 26 & lifted all illegal drugs from me. It is 10:30 A.M. & I want to be young pretty, & well again. We'll take it! I was 2 years old crying over my grandmother's house & mammy said she was going to get a peach tree switch. I said mammy but that is not a peach tree & she did not whip me. I wanted my turtle & foo foo fooler. She used to cook norsters - oysters, steak, fish, vegetable soup, potato candy, Christmas cookies, & sew all my clothes. Mammy did not drink anything but coca-cola, coffee, buttermilk & cornbread. Both mother & mammy were good cooks. I cannot cook like that! A way to a man's heart is thru his stomach. Cooking will not get you into Heaven. You spat on cousin Faith's grave for murdering my child & telling me to go to the food bank. You are so jealous of hippy girlfriend Gift/gifted that died at 49. She was a good Pisces & your best friend with beautiful long brown hair - guitarist. Alexis was the sweetest switch board operator at Camel Carriers Trucking Company. Black Horse to see the Chippendales on her daughter's 21st birthday. Alexis was diabetic & went blind.

She was the kindest person in the world. A man died from an inoperable brain tumor - he is up in Heaven. Honesty died in the sunshine state. He said there was not a mean bone in your body. Honesty got employee of the month & had plants everywhere. His sister died from an operation. The doctor cut a hole in her stomach.

Humility was funny & we went to Gatlinburg, TN in the winter, West Louisville bar, & drank rum & coke, story teller, single dances. God sees everything! Her best friend was born on Halloween & died from cancers Paul used to write me letters & died from aides. He owes me money. Paul was a con-artist. He was put in jail & you had better not _____ him. Paul was a piano genius & Lazerus was such a talented guy. That was when your mother died from throat cancer & she was such a bitch. You were a scapegoat. Eve was the religious nurse & your mother had morphine & dilaudid. You are a piece of SH#T Mae. You had better thank God for another day. You cannot stand to look in the mirror. Persistance was a LEO RN nurse - your best friend. We went to Girl Scout camp, & snuck men in. We canoed the green river twice, White River, smoked pot, cigarettes, hopped bars, went to a psychic awareness convention. She has 2 beautiful boys! How long has she been gone? You were whores, sluts, & bitches. True/Trust/Truth was your best Scorpio friend - there's a concert on cloud nine. Why did God make tornadoes, hurricanes? Lord, have mercy! Mercy died in a fire after she got busted for drugs, and her son accidently shot himself & died. Take Mercy to your shrink. Do something Christian. She is Cuban. Aunt Abundance was a saint, poured milk on Faith's head, had a big, rich $500,000 house, a condo in the Bahamas, broke her hip twice & knew how to shoot a gun. She said that the vet's son who shot himself in front of his wife & child was evil. Forgiveness, my best girlfriend is going to grab that dead mother _____er up & beat the SH#T out of him.

Aunt Abundance gave me an angel, Oceana. I miss her most of all! Were they snobs? The purple rain is psychedelic. Oh, how I am scared, phobia of purple rain. God blessed the poor. Forgiveness told her deceased ex-husband, Disobedience to cram all his money up his ass. Disobedience died at 40 from drinking.

You cannot bull SH#T a bull SH#TTER. Do not touch him! His best friend, died at 60, also a drinker, on an oxygen Julie & I dated him. Cast a spell on him! Make snow angels! He was a good man! You are going to cast a spell on that chocolate devil's food cake. God works in mysterious ways. Messiah, the gay organist at beloved Hebrew Tabernacle is dead & so is Sarah Israel. May light perpetual shine upon them. Cheer, my black soul sister wanted to sue me for having the word nigger in my book, Jeans/genes. What kind of disease did she have? All she wanted was the food stamp card & money. She got fired from Shop-a-Lot #666 #999 for stealing & now she rests in peace. A black nigger in a neighboring town thru gasoline on the car salesman Bugar & set him on fire. He got off! You had better not drink vodka & water. Andy died from alheimers just like Uncle Humor. Aunt Wisdom died from cancer of the spleen. They were your favorites. Eat protein. I know Jack SHIT! Her last words to me were do not sell the house & do not have children. They will come back to me & get me out of this hell hole. They were a Libra & a Gemini - very compatible. Eat popsicles & watch T.V. Uncle Humor was an insurance salesman & took me everywhere. They have a boat in Hollywood, FL named the Billy Marie. Do not touch anything at Tiffany's. Look at Sea World - riding orca whales, seals, dolphins, & sharks.

They have a dalmatian named Yorka & a black collie named Sneakers. My job was to walk them.

Aunt Wisdom taught me how to crochet. When the ocean was rough, I used to straddle the raft & ride the waves, drank wine, & kissed a boy named Steve - a hippy with long beautiful hair. Mom pulled my hair in Atlanta airport. You had better not touch that ham! Aunt Wisdom sewed just like mammy & had arthritis in her hands. Armaggedon was a junkie that got killed by a drunk driver. He begged me to be with him & would not marry me. He wanted to make sure the shoe fit first. Love od'd on morphine. Her brother, Fear that went to Lagrange for armed robbery drowned. Venzuela od'd on Mother's Day a year after her son o'd. That is the saddest thing I have ever heard from her ex-husband, Gideon, who I lived with in 1982. Venzuela was the prettiest girl in Zion, Egypt High School & believed in God. Mourn & weep, Maebelle, Revelations, Laughter, Perseverence, Red Sea, Bishop, Pope are all dead. Compassion is compassion. Angel I & Isabella are dead. Jehosaphat is dead. Sacrifice who shot himself in the head is dead. Only the good die young. You have to go thru hell before you get to Heaven. There are homeless people that break your heart. Czekoslavia is the prettiest bride you ever saw. Her husband Poland passed away - a good man. Those that save their life will lose it and those that lose their life for Jesus Christ's sake will save it. Where is love. Does it fall from the skies above? Is it underneath the willow tree that I've been dreaming of? I have one male doll - Zachary Oliver named after my good-looking therapist - Dr. Mosiah who is good with children & says I have delusions. Have an enchanting day - the most beautiful fairy. I have ever seen - Jaborwocky. I cannot stand the name Alice. - Alice in Wonderland - the good queen & the bad queen - Off with their heads. Tweedle dee Tweedle dum The majors at the Amazing Marines were funny & absolute saints.

He said you'll get to Heaven for saying SH#T but you won't get to Heaven for saying. God _____. They have a beautiful farm, cabin, horses, donkey named Azaelah - spared from Jehovah, cows. & you had better not cuss. Cunt is the nastiest word you can say. Candle, candle, all aglow, tell me what you know. Ask & you shall receive, seek & you shall find. Knock & the door will be opened to you. Now, I have to wear a stupid kidney dialysis belt for my catheder - Job Taurus 5-10 is my favorite drug mafia cousin. What if he dies? You will be so sad. The Bible is sacred no matter what Canaan says. My God is not a _____ing asshole. He means everything to me. Thank You for another day. You've always taken care of me & my friend. How are Thee? Amen. Robin Williams was manic-depressive funny, famous & he hung himself. Did he go to hell for that? How many commandments have you broken? Are you anorexic? You had better stay alive long enough to get queen Goddess of the office written. Penance do a good deed to make-up for the bad per cheer, soul sister. God loves you! You promised me Heaven but you put me thru hell. You give love a bad name. The child's name is Season Marie Rapheal named after an angel. Is this real? You made a deal, - no drinking & driving. Who is Mr. Star? Your car got stolen - brown century buick - joy riding because you left the keys in your car. You keep losing your car & purse in your dreams. Beware of Karma! Life after death. Look what happened to the Beatles, John Lennon. Poncho was so talented & commited suicide. Hotch got electrocuted by putting an aluminum ladder to turn the lights on. His beautiful sister died young from breast cancer & her brother Garbage is dead. You danced at Aaron's & True/Trust/Truth's wedding. Forgiveness & True/Trust/Truth both got abortions & have no remorse. These boots are made for walking & I'll tell you what to do. One of these days these boots are going to stomp all over you. Uncle Protection died from lung cancer & his nephew died from cirrhosis of the liver. You had better not drink moonshine. My piano teacher passed away. Fabel, my best friend in High School died. We used to do mescaline, acid, cocaine together. Dr. Fabel thought he was possessed by the devil & shot himself - a good dentist. Obedience died in a car wreck. Her mother mean Jeanne was so talented. They lost 3 children & their house was a mess. You look just like Obedience & you are not laughing. Father Klon was Catholic & thru a fit when all this rich ladie's money inheritance went to her lover & not the church. Your mother got her feelings hurt. I don't believe Jesus was a Capricorn. I think He was a Taurus born in May. God said maybe. You wanted that baby. Peace was agnostic, a great art teacher & she is bitchy dead. Des parado. You make your mother sick. Come shoot this ghost! Sometimes I just sit & think & sometimes I just sit. Lead, follow, or get out of the way. Ecclesiastes, the gay lesbian alcoholic has passed away. How did the coroner get my telephone number? You have a big _____ing house, what do I have? You get on my _____ing nerves. & you're negative. Ecclesiastes name was in the Bible & it meant star. She was Episcopalian, did not go to Church; but, talked to God every day. She lost her house all because of 53th 3rd bank & her best friend Happiness spent her $7,000 disability back pay. What about her Jack Russell dogs & cat? Mae needs more faith. France died from cirrhosis of the liver. She was so pretty with red hair, brown eyes, & had 2 beautiful girls, one who cut all her hair off.

I sent a bereavement card & got a thank-you note. I thought that was nice. Mae rolls with the punches. My nickname is Lee Lamb & I am a lamb of God. Oh Lamb of God that takest away the sins of the world, have mercy upon us. Oh, Lamb of God that takest away the sins of the world, grant us thy peace. Ecclesiastes cussed, cursed like a sailor, did not like Hidden Hills, the _____ing police were up there every day & now can see everything I do in spirit. Do lesbians that have been raped go to Heaven? Read Leviticus. Another one has bit the dust. Ecclesiastes had black hair, green eyes, & rotten teeth. I loved her! Scorpio Joy could not stand Gemini Ecclesiastes. There are ghosts everywhere! Crucifixion was so cruel. Jesus was beat, stabbed, fed vinegar. Set behind me, satan. Are there mermaids in the Atlantic ocean like in Pirates of the Caribean? Ecclesiastes did not like Johnny Depp but I love him! Heaven is your home. You had better get a cross tattoo on your arm or back. I AM THAT I AM. Theology, my brindle tabby cat is the cutest, sweetest child I have ever had. I could not stand the blood in Stephen King's movie IT. I cannot stand scammers, pedifiles & rapists. Damascus has a feeding tube. Pray for him! We both are not ready to die. All my friends are flakes. Get off of my cloud nine. You had better say that Lord's prayer. You had better say a prayer for the damned.

TRUE CONFESSIONS
ANGER
Psalm 80

Restore us, O God of Hosts; show the light of your countenance, and we will be saved.
O Lord God of hosts, how long will you be angered despite the prayers of your people?
You have fed them with the bread of tears; you have given them bowls of tears to drink.
You have made us the derision of our neighbors; and our enemies laugh us to scorn.
Why do you say peace when there is no peace?
Why do you say mercy when there is no mercy?
Why do you say love when there is no love?
Why do you say hope when there is no hope?
Why do you say joy when there is no joy?
Why do you say cheer when there is no cheer?
Why do you say happiness when we are unhappy?
Why do you say solice when there is anger?
Why do you make crazy people - murderers?
Why do make pedifiles?
Why do you allow child abuse?
Why do you make criminals, rapists?
Why do you curse us night & day?
Why do you let Satan test, tempt us?

The anger, lightning bolts of hate, the wrath of God. Vengeance is mine saith the Lord. Anger is detrimental to my blessed loving soul. Why do you say God is love? Mary & Mary Magdeline are bitter, angry at the cruelty Jesus went thru on Calvary nailed to the cross. There's got to be a better way than this in your world.

Why do you say calm when all there is is fear? Why do you let dark angels kill us?

Yours very truly,
Tawny "Mae" Harris
Gypsy Sky
Azul Celeste

P.S. I hate to be so negative; but anger is flooding, drowning my being. Why do you say prosperity when there are hungry & diseases.

Thank you for your candle-lighting faith. I AM coming down to save you from poverty & hate.

This crucifies all my ex-lovers by graphically telling what they did to me in bed. Sex in the city. All my X's live in Texas. What does God say about sex? I've had some good lovers. I've been thru diamonds & mines - love stinks.

This is going to be just like Fifty Shades of Grey - a best seller.

Dicks, penises are where men's brains are located. I love Lorana Bobbit! There were 2 men in a car & something splat on the window. Did you see the dick on that bug? A man tattooed his dick with a $100 bill because women like to blow money. Mae was a whore, bitch, & a slut. Whores make the best wives. You were a free prostitute just like Mary Magdeline that Jesus cast 7 demons out of her. You are not a fake Christian. LOVE all ends in a confusing laugh. Why do you say heaven when everything is hell? Eat an egg to change your luck. Beware of Pisces.

When I was 13, I had a boyfriend with blonde hair & puppy dog brown eyes, Wonderful Advisor. He gave me a sweet heart ring, was head basketball star, & I was head cheerleader. All we did was kiss & I should have stayed with him.

I LONG O VONG E U. That's when my beloved grandmother died & I turned to drugs & alcohol. I loved his mother. Mom said someone will get a divorce, you're better off without him, you're a martyr, a greedy gut, ingrates, snarley garley old lady, fat hog, poor pitiful pearl, & to count your blessings. Oh, she also called me slut. She was a bitch! Now, I am an old maid on disability with kidney dialysis - no sex for me.

Wonderful Advisor & I had a beautiful platonic relationship & he holds a special place in my heart. His 2nd marriage, he is married to a girl that looks like Sarah Jessica Parker & they have a smart beautiful 8 year old girl. He has 2 grown boys from his 1st marriage. We do not talk much anymore but the puppy love is there. We were a popular couple. Mom liked Wonderful Advisor. Why did we break up?

All we did is kiss. Why did God make lice, maggots! Ticks, fleas, roaches? In Zion, Egypt Jr. High School, there was this mean black nigger girl that was going to beat Forgiveness & me up. She got exspelled. After a game one night, we walked to a phone at a store for our parents to pick us up. Those mother _____ing niggers threw a rock & hit Mediterranean Sea in the head. Blood was all over my hand. Two of the higher class black people apologized. I loved them for that! You had to eat in the cafeteria & the spaghetti was terrible. When I was 15 at Girl Scout camp, we snuck men in. This blonde haired good-looking boy stripped me in a field. I said, "I thought you did not do this till you got married." He said, "that's what you think." When my best friend, Persistance & I canoed the Green River, we went to an amusement park in Bowling Green, broke into a cabin, drank, smoked pot, laughed. I gave my first blow job to a boy I did not know with a huge, hard dick. All the counselors got fired. When I was 16, St. Peter Eater rode me hard & I lost a pint of blood on a white bedspread. I dated St. Peter many times & he raped me each time we went out & said I gave the best blow jobs in town. A lady from Camel Carriers & I had a threesome & I went first & then he socked it to her with a huge dildo - voyeurism. I taped a note on the door - TOO KINKY - NOT COMING.

St. Peter Eater was a drummer & Elvis Impersonator. The best date I ever had was when we went to a bar club, called a friend from Girl Scout Camp, danced & watched him sing & play the drums. I dressed up in pink. Mother used to say, "Did you _____ him?" That is none of her business. Chickie pierced my ears with white silver gold balls. Mother said I could not go to Texas to visit Gift/gifted, Pope & his wife. My beloved grandmother & I did not know how to get the earrings out of my ears. I got to go to Corpus, Christi, TX & Lorado, MX. There were beggars with no arms or legs. The Mexicans like blondes. I bought a stuffed snake, iguana, & tiger eye ring. Pope & mother bought liquor. I was 13 & that's when I started smoking Doral cigarettes. I wish I had never started. Mother, Loyal Dedication said pierced earrings made you wild as horses. You cannot drink the water in Mexico. We went to the beach & saw the original cast of Jesus Christ Superstar where St. Caiphas tells Jesus to walk across the swimming pool. We had fun! Gift/gifted was a hippy, could really play the guitar & died at 49 they say from cancer. I want to go to her grave & talk to her.

What happened? When I was in Zion, Egypt High School, I used to double date with good-looking Disobedience & Forgiveness. Disobedience was freaking out at the lights of a car & wanted to know if I wanted to do junk. I dated several of his good friends but did not go to bed with them. All we did was drink & smoke pot. Disobedience died at 40. Forgiveness married him & had a beautiful girl named Saducee. Saducee had 6 children that she does not take good care of. Forgiveness divorced Disobedience & told him to cram all his money up his ass. Forgiveness went to prison for 2 years for D.U.I.'s & counterfeiting 20's. She cusses like a sailor. I dated Monk, Lazerus & aborted his child. We were the perfect couple & I loved him & prayed for his soul every night. He is in a half-way house up in Heaven for suicide. Oh, how I wish I could have had that baby! Then along came Jordan, Thaddeus with a big dick who used to say suck my pud. He almost got fired from his mining job for sending a naked picture of himself to a girl & saying he was good in bed. I chased him for 2 years & Rev. Daniels said he was the one I should have married. Thaddeus used to sell cocaine; but, now he is a teacher at the Lavender Forever Baptist

Church. Canaan cannot stand Jordan Thaddeus; but, I loved him very much. Would I have divorced him for that? Thaddeus sent me 2 dozen peach roses & finally called me for a date when there was a foot of snow. I said no. Are you crazy? I was watching the movie Reincarnation of Peter Proud. His father was a wealthy man & he lost his adopted brother. That has been years ago at the Zion, Egypt Community College. I met Josiah, a red-haired lawyer at his wedding. Oh, how I sucked Josiah's dick until it got hard. He ate me pulling my labia flabia growths in his mouth, licked my butt & blew on it. Josiah was good in bed. Then along came Gideon. We drank makers Mark Jack Black Jack Green in my apartment in Brown Town in 1982 & _____ed like rabbits. I threw up shrimp giving him a blow job & he finger _____ed me to death. Gideon married another bitch he got pregnant. I was 24. That's when Cain, Abel's brother raped me.

I was drunk & all I remember is his big dick riding me. Cain's friend got shot & killed duck hunting. I was so promiscous. How many times have I been used?

One madre pod me hum - meditate on those candles. Mae has had some really good lovers. I was put in jail twice for a D.U.I. that was dropped & placed in House of Horrors/Wax for manic-depression & paranoid schizophrenia. That's where I met Isaiah who wanted to marry me; but, the preacher wouldn't do it. He said if one got sick, the other one could not hold them up. They put me back on the deadly lithium. Mother liked Isaiah. Isaiah said if he were gay, he would be with your brother, Micah. I thought that was nice. In my first nice apartment I had sex all the time. Romans had elephantitis he was so big. I gave him a blow job. He cummed in my mouth & I threw up. Persistance & I used to pick men up in bars. We were free whores & we went out on Thunder on the Ohio with one of your dates & got burnt to a crisp. I went to the bar & this man with a wad of money in his hand bought me a drink & started fondling my leg. I immediately got up & went outside yelling for Persistance who was at the boat dock with the boat owner date. We were young, dumb, & full of cum. A girl at the apartment got pregnant & wanted a butcher knife to cut it out of her belly. I had to hide the knife & she got an abortion. The owner of the apartments shot himself because he was in so much pain with cancer. This was in 1981. I had 3 jobs - Mom's Real Estate & cleaning offices. The apartment was furnished for $175 a month & I cried when I had to move back home. I had 2 female girlfriends roommates that moved away that I loved. Maebelle took mom to Las Vegas. Look at the shooting that happened down there. Why did God make germs? Rubbers are nasty! Why did God make bats & rats? You had better not mess around with Mother Nature. Why did God make spiders & snakes? You had better not tread on me. Pray for your crazy family. Is God a jerk? No, God is loving-kindness. He cannot stand violence. Jesus is in the tribe of Judah. Gay brother Micah is impotent from drinking vodka & orange juice & has got the littlest 4 inch dick you have ever seen. When I worked at a clothing factory, a bi-sexual queen got shot in the head & killed. How many tricks do you have in your hand - spades, Rook. You had better not shake a baby. The police know what kind of car you drive when you had to pay $100 for hitting a mailbox at the 50th class reunion. You did not drink a drop & you have night blindness. The black policeman wanted you to put your German Shepherd husky, Calvin Klein up. The jerk neighbor made me give her away to the Humane Society. Why did God make horse flies? Judge & be judged not. The wicked get no rest until they close their eyes for good. Candle, candle all aglow, tell me what you know. May God give you strength when yours is gone.

May His grace & mercy
Carry you on,
May the unending love
That He has for you
Revive your heart
And see you through

In 1982 - bad year - I got off my lithium & used to go to an illegal bar. There was a girl dressed in camoflage who got beat in Detroit & a broken coke bottle crammed up her vagina severing her fallopian tubes. She milked her breasts so I showed my breasts & a man bit my titty. I then got naked & showed my clitoris on a pool table. You can look but you cannot touch. That is the sluttiest thing I have ever done. That's when I was living with Gideon. I wanted to work as dishwasher at the bar. Gideon got fired for drinking & his father passed away. He drove an orange truck & got all his teeth knocked out in a wreck. I went to House of Horrors/Wax where I met Isaiah. I am living on a prayer. Oh God our help in ages past. Our hope for years to come. Who saved us from the stormy blast & helped us to live on. Gideon went to Volta House for his drinking. That was a horrible place. That's when I read God calling for 25 years. Only scarred lives save. Religion is witchery in the wrong hands. Kill self now. I was living in poverty & it was around. Halloween. I was not pregnant. I was locked-up with murderers & thieves & almost got raped twice. Look what your bitch mother did to you. I am not a devil! I am not satan's daughter. A month & a half of hell. You cannot stand to have an arm put around you & you cannot stand to be touched. Why did God make hornets & wasps? Give me silver, blue, & gold, the color of the sky I'm told. My rainbow is overdue. Gideon butt _____ed me & I screamed. Rainbow was my big calico guinea pig that I had for 4 years. Then came along Penecostal, a long pencil dick, goat _____er that dumped me for an ex-girlfriend. Was he on drugs, a mailman. Did he steal social security checks? Then came along Bartholomew who looked like Jesus from behind. Magic candle of the world, all your mysterious come unfurled. All the sorrow, all the regret. There are some things I'll never forget.

Run with the devil, gone with the wind. Cursing & swearing is a sin. Where the hell is my car? All these dead people's spirits are so afar. You have dreamed dreams about God, Jesus, & angels will they all come true? You are a reincarnated Mary Magdeline. All of your friends are true blue.

Smoking is going to kill you if you don't quit. Mother Loyal Dedication is throwing a fit. Oh, SH#T! Kidney dialysis is a bitch. Politics suck! Ditch Mitch! I don't believe in abortion except for incest, rape & mental retardation & if the pregnancy will kill the mother. Prostitutes & tax collectors will go to Heaven because they believed per Matthew. You are married to Jesus Christ, a carpenter - a bride of the Lord. Amanda down at the Amazing Marines Soldier of the cross was wiccan. How many gods are there? God of the East, God of the west, God of the north, & God of the south. You had better shut your mouth. You have been an absolute angel since God talked to you. Genesis, deceased Faith's husband said he sold his soul & God gave him another one. Sprinkle, sprinkle fairy dust Pisces bitch who aborted my child & told me to go to the food bank when I was starving. Our Lady of Mercy was all her fault. When I was in Zion, Egypt High School, I wanted a German Shepherd puppy. I took him to the vet to get the lice off him. His name was Stuffin. I was changing Faith's cute son Leviticus's diaper & the dog chewed his tiny wing wang & brought blood. Faith was putting on her make-up & did not know. I had to get rid of Stuffin because mom wouldn't let me keep him. I lost money on the dog. Leviticus's dick is fine for he now has 2 beautiful children. I felt bad! I was babysitting & giving Leviticus a bath, Samson, his older brother stuck a large bobby pin up his butthole, ass. I should have whipped him; but I didn't. Puerta Rica whom I loved got a divorce & now Samson & Delilah are getting a divorce. They have 2 darling sons. His oldest son is going to college to major in political science. They are both good Christian boys. Penecostal girls are the prettiest, dressed up to a tie & long beautiful hair. I feel uneasy in their church talking in tongues. I have had bad sex & I have had good sex. Bartholomew snaggle tooth was the best sex I have ever had. I used to drive to the truck stop in my yellow Impala after work on 2nd shift at Camel Carriers Trucking Company. He had a 7 year common law wife & lived in the country up north. I am really going to crucify this truck driver because I had feelings for him. My heart's not made of rubber. My soul's not made of glass & if you break my heart & soul, I am going to kick your ass. I used to ride his big hard dick & put him to sleep in the bed of his oily truck. Bad to the bone. I would stir my bourbon & sprite with his dick. Getting dressed, I would let myself out of the truck & the other trucks would blink their lights. I am not a lot lizard! Mom called me a slut & I moved into an efficiency apartment for $125 a month. Bartholomew & I used to make beautiful love on the mattress on the floor & he would buy me groceries - straight suck & _____ & sucking toes. He had nail rot. He said I could cook 'bout as good as I _____

63

ed. He broke up with me & I moved back home to help mom pay the taxes. I lived in this apartment for 6 months & they gave me a house hold shower that I greatly appreciated. I dated Bartholomew for 4 years & he went thru 3 blondes during the time I worked for the company for 17 years blind diabetic sweet Alexis being one of them. Then along came Paul, the genius piano player con artist who died from aides. Here is his first note he wrote me from jail. It was a beautiful sweet Valentine's homemade card - no candy, no lingerie, just a little piece of me. We wrote each other for a year while he was in St. Francis of Assissi. Paul had a small dick & I miss him. God sent me to him & I will be very blessed for that. I threw away all the cards so my next boyfriend would not find the love letters. I used to send him roses & made him a beautiful pointilism of him & his son playing the piano. Oh, where have all my friends gone? Now, I am on home kidney dialysis & I am afraid of dying. Micah, my gay brother wants to know what I am living for. I am living for my cat Theology & Tangerine.

That is mean. I went celebant for 12 years after that then along came Benjamin, the married man I have committed adultery 3 times & he finger _____ed me. I sucked the life out of his dick masterbating. Then along came Satan another married man who begged me to go to bed with him. He had the littliest penis & big balls. It hurt so bad & brought blood. He is scum of the Earth. I had to go to the Health Department for a yeast infection & genital warts, HIV test & paps smear. You have had the SH#T raped out of you. There is a butterfly on your finger. You lost a good friend, funny miracle. Be of good cheer, Jesus has overcomed the world. Then came Jayden "Care" Arthur that was too young for you. Did his mother die? Mae has been tested way too hard. Pray hard! What is wrong with your mind - chemical imbalance in your brain. Sunshine & air is the balm for all ills. Cast a spell. Spread the word. Mae is a flower child - hippy. I know, you know, I know. Nobody knows when Jesus is coming back from the East. Micah was a mean, mean little boy. He is so silly! The Amazing Marines Soldiers of the cross breaks my heart - poor white trash - good people. Volunteer of the year. My God is the greatest God there is. The Beatitudes are my favorite, Blessed are the poor in spirit for they will see God. Blessed are the peacemakers for they are the children of God. Blessed are the meek they will inherit the Earth. Blessed are they that mourn for they will laugh. Your alcoholic mother is driving you insane. You would have committed suicide if she was still alive. Casper is a friendly ghost.

Uncle Protection almost raped you when you were drinking. I am not Baba! I am not Baba! Aunt Beautiful Patience was the kindest, gentliest soul. Turn the other cheek. You almost killed yourself twice working at Shop-a-Lot #666. How many times have you been stabbed in the back. I can do all things thru Christ that strengthens me. You could have sued Shop-a-Lot. LOVE castest out all fear. You are not vain. Jesus loves you this I know because the Bible tells us so. Red, yellow, black, white. All are precious in his sight. God is on your side. You followed that white gloved hand everywhere.

SCREAM FOR ICE CREAM

Door of Hope is praying for you.
Women do it for love
Men do it for pleasure.

You are scared of sex. Trista in French means one night stand. I cannot stand amoré or Jezreel. That firing was a blessing in disguise. You had to take care of Compassion who was a Sagistarius & died of lung cancer. Oh, Lord open my eyes to see what is beautiful. My mind to know what is true. My heart to love what is good. For Christ's sake. Amen.

Andrew was my favorite. He was schizophrenic & we used to go eat steak & okra. We went to see The Prophecy & I held his hand. He thought the police were putting pot in his car. I would not kiss him & he went home & shot himself. Andrew was unstable. It is finished. Those gay guys called Micah a bitch & a mother _____er, got in his bed, stole his liquor & now friends with them. The older gay guy passed away. He was a beautician & his counter part is sending religious cards that I am so thankful to get. Micah called the police & they almost went to jail. What if St. Peter was by your bed? Do you want to come back as a chicken or a dog? The man said a chicken & was laying an egg. His wife said wake up Henry, your crapping all over the bed! A little boy was gingerly thumbing thru the Bible & found a leaf. He said look mom what I found - Adam's suit. There was a man that went to a prostitute. The prostitute said $25 $50 $100. The man said will you pee in a cup for a quarter and she did. He took the cup of pee downstairs, stuck his penis in it & said drink soup you son-of-a-bitch meat's too high. Abraabra cadabra I want to reach out & grab ya. Hocus pokus! Your body is your temple. Your hair is your glory. Christ has died. Christ has risen. Christ will come again. Happy Easter!

This SCREAM FOR ICE CREAM is all made up of jokes to make you laugh. LOVE & LAUGH!

A little boy was at his grandmother's house & the preacher came to the door. The TV television did not work & the little boy said she was banging on her boyfriend. Do you smoke after sex? I don't know, I've never looked. A little boy threw some aspirin out a bus window. My ass burns! My ass burns! Stick it out the window & cool it off! What do they call 2 gay guys named Bob? Oral Roberts. Rub a dub, dub, thanks for the grub. Yeah, God!

George Washington cut down the cherry tree in Texas & told his father he could not tell a lie. His father said we are moving to Virginia because if you cannot tell a lie, you'll never make it in Texas. Why do I keep getting my purse lost, stolen in my dreams? Red sky at night. Sailors delight. Red sky in morning. Sailors warning. The tip came off my catheder - more bad luck. 0700 9-28-20. It is bad luck to be born a duck. Conjunction, conjunction - what's your function. It is raining. It is pouring, the old man is snoring. I have such a phobia of purple rain. Cold hands, warm heart. Pumpkins, witches, warlocks, sorcerors come on Halloween night, Costumes, treats or tricks - full of mischief & fright. Throwing eggs, soaping windows - dressed to kill Happy Halloween throughout the year. 2020 - Covid 19 corona virus is getting on my last nerve. We are placed here on this Earth to serve. This world is crazy when autumn is near. Black cats, brooms love casteth out all fear. Razors in apples, pins in cookies - cruel pranks. You had better be saved before the rapture - army tanks. White heavenly beings angels see all the good & the bad. You can call your Holy Father Dad. Dressed as ghosts, devils, princesses - all wanting a treat - smell of my feet - give me something good to eat. Spread the word, the word became flesh. I like Jesus Christ my savior the best. He is coming like a thief in the night, riding a white horse, white hair aflowing. There had better not be #6 on your hand. Meteorites, trials & tribulations Mae's faith is growing.

Heaven or bust. Jayden was lust. St. Peter's gates will open for all his saints to come thru. God, Jesus, the Holy Spirit cares for me & you. Purple acid raindrops, dinosaur tears, then the sunshine comes out. All your friends have died, in Heaven you have clout Hells bells, thunder shack you had better watch your back. Voices come & go - they put you down, tell you what to do.

I am so tired of being snobbed & called stupid by people like you. Be careful what you wish for. You may end up in my novel, that's a fact.

Satan, Lucifer, devil, beast is so vain. Why is there so much suffering & pain? You are brown nosing God because He means so much to me. On home kidney dialysis, all you do is urinate, pee. You want to go to Salem where the witches are, New York City, Colorado, Pennsylvania, Israel all on a trip, Scotland, when I die & go to Heaven, I can travel in spirit. HO LEE CH#T. God's world is so beautiful, magnificent. Isabella, Compassion, Cheer, Angel I, Ecclesiastes deceased will always be in my heart & soul. It's not my time to go! Haunted houses, jailhouse rock. God has perfect timing - look at the clock. Gypsy Sky, Azul Celeste - I am wanted dead or alive. Be a good sumaritan, philaprophist, helper, healer, teacher, preacher, evangeliest, prophet - talk in tongues. There was this city boy who wanted to hunt on a farm. The farmer said do not shoot any farm animals. The city boy shot a goat & ran up to the farmhouse. I shot a hard head with horns, beard & stuck. The farmer said, "Oh, hell, you have killed my wife." You are petrified of goth. A sweet 80 year old lady found a package of condoms that said keep wet, place on organ, prevents disease: so, she put the condom in a bowl of water & placed it on top of the organ. Her preacher came to visit her & asked her about it. She said she hasn't been sick all year. Why did God not like black people? He put pubic hair on their heads. LOVE & LAUGH. Laughter is good medicine. Look up, look down, look all around. Your pants are falling down. Diarhea cha cha cha you may think it's funny but it's really black & runny. Faty, faty 2 x 4 couldn't get thru the bathroom door, pissed in the floor & did it some more. There was this man that went to a bar & nobody paid any attention to him. He went to a barber & said dye my hair black still nobody paid any attention so he went back to the barber and said put a blue streak, green streak, red streak, purple streak, orange streak, yellow streak in my hair. He went back to the bar & a man was staring at him. The man said, "what's wrong with you, haven't you ever seen a man before?" The old man said I screwed, _____ed a peacock once & I thought maybe you were my son. The grossest joke I ever heard was this man who ate mayonnaise & the jar was empty & got filled every night so he woke up & watched a man squeeze pus from his zits into the jar. You had better tell your favorite Aunt Beautiful Patience you're sorry. She did not eat mayonnaise for a week. Ezekiel said people were eating SH#T on the computer, Jayden was having sex with 12 year olds & afternoon delights. You cannot stand Free Will's long skinny dick with big pie pan. You had better have pussy control. Free will almost married a black lady. If you go black, you'll never go back. What would you do if your child did acid, mescaline, pot, junk, heroin? Japan, Mom's junkie nurse friend said, "you had better not mam me!" She was an Aquarius born on my birthday January 21 on the cusp with Capricorn. That Aquarius song by the 5th Dimension was #1 for 5 weeks. Are Aquarius's psychic? Tell God a joke. Laughter was your beloved step mother that passed away at 91. She was in assistant living & said the food was terrible. God works in mysterious ways & she is with my dad, Perseverence. Laughter was a beautiful Libra - very compatible with Aquarius. Libra is the most beautiful sign, then Aquarius. Laughter had a beautiful daughter who had 3 beautiful girls. Prayer is the wireless connection. Wac Dad a dead beat Dad? Did he give a hoot. You always go back to the one that abuses you - your parents did not get along. When your mother & father forsake you then I will lift you up. What if your child o'd on codeine? Would you do Meth? Mae saw Godspell on acid - blue microdot, purple microdot, blotter, sunshine, LSD 25. Godspell is Free Will's mother & I love her. She is the most beautiful Capricorn in the world. Trump or Biden? This country United States of America is in deep SH#T. A teacher asks 3 boys if you were on a date how to excuse yourself to go to the restroom. The 1st boy said, "I have to go pee!" The teacher said, "that is inappropriate." The 2nd boy said, "I have to go to the bathroom." The teacher said, "that's not nice." Then little Johnny said, "I have to shake hands with an old friend that I hope to introduce to you after dinner." There was an 80 year old lady & she went to the doctor & the doctor said you're in perfect health, do you have sex? The old lady said I don't know I'll have to ask my husband; so, she goes to the waiting room & screams, "Henry, do we have sex?!" The waiting room went quiet, hushed. Then Henry says, "no Edna I've told you a million times, we have blue cross, blue shield. There was this girl & it was her 50th birthday. She went to a hardware store - "It's my birthday, guess how old I am." 24. No, 50. She went to MacDonalds'." Its my birthday, guess how old I am!" 35, No. 50. By this time, she is feeling pretty good about herself. She is sitting on a bench waiting for the bus & there's an old man sitting next to her. "Its my birthday, guess how old I am!"

The old man said, "my eyesight is poor; but, if you let me fondle your breasts, I'll tell you how old you are. So the girl said, what the hell." He fondled her breasts & said 50. The girl said how did you know. The old man said he was standing behind you in the line at MacDonalds. There was this older couple & their daughter had just been inaugurated as President of the United States. The girl calls her parents to come up & see her at her speech. The mother says we don't drive. The daughter says I will send you a limosine. The mother says we have nothing to wear. The daughter says I will buy you the finest clothes from New York City. The older couple are sitting at the inaugeration speech in Washington, D.C. & the older man turns to a congressman & says see that girl up there giving a speech, her brother played basketball for U.K. There was this lady & her tightwad husband died. She bought a Cadillac & mink coat when she went to get his urn of ashes. She came home & poured the ashes on the table. Henry, see that car you always promised, me - it's in the garage. See that mink coat you always promised me - I've got it on. Remember, that blow job you always wanted. W-H-O-O-S-H she blows the ashes off the table. Milk, milk, lemonade, around the corner fudge is made. To the left, to the left, to the right, to the left. My back is breaking. My bras too tight, my boobs are shaking from left to right. I hope this SCREAM FOR ICE CREAM has cheered you up in these turbulant times. God wants you to prosper, love & laugh.

Printed in the United States
by Baker & Taylor Publisher Services